# THE HOLY GHOST GOT A NEW DANCE

# THE HOLY GHOST GOT A NEW DANCE

An Examination of Black Theology and
Holy Hip-hop in Inner-City Ministry

## WILLIE HUDSON

Foreword by Don Thorsen

RESOURCE *Publications* · Eugene, Oregon

THE HOLY GHOST GOT A NEW DANCE
An Examination of Black Theology and Holy Hip-hop in Inner-City
Ministry

Resource Publications
An Imprint of Wipf and Stock Publishers
199 W. 8th Ave., Suite 3
Eugene, OR 97401

www.wipfandstock.com

PAPERBACK ISBN: 978-1-5326-0453-9
HARDCOVER ISBN: 978-1-5326-0455-3
EBOOK ISBN: 978-1-5326-0454-6

Manufactured in the U.S.A.                    OCTOBER 24, 2016

*This work is dedicated to my mother, Patsy*

# Contents

# Foreword

*By Don Thorsen*

THERE OCCUR MANY CHALLENGES in Christian ministry, and those challenges increase dramatically in urban contexts that are multiracial, multiethnic, and multicultural. Willie Hudson draws upon decades of urban ministerial experience with both adults and youth, which has benefited from his implementation of principles from Black Theology and his appreciation for hip-hop music and culture. In particular, Hudson is concerned about ministering to youth, focusing upon youth who are black and brown, since they are especially susceptible to misrepresentations and injustices in contemporary society.

Too often Christians have been fearful of Black Theology, but their fears may come from ignorance or misassociations, rather than from the lack of Black Theology's grounding in biblical teaching. Black theologians such as James Cone are pioneers in talking about the situatedness (or contextuality) of our lives, that is, how our daily beliefs, values, and practices are influenced by our personal and social backgrounds. Sometimes the particular circumstances of our backgrounds strengthen our Christianity; other times our backgrounds weaken it. Ignoring our situatedness makes us susceptible to cultural forces—knowingly or unknow-ingly—that may frustrate and treat people unjustly. Cone especial-ly points out how people, including Christians, become neglected, marginalized, and oppressed due to their race and/or ethnicity. So, if ministry in multicultural (or intercultural) urban contexts is to be successful, then Christians need to be aware of and minister empathetically to the diverse racial, ethnic, and cultural backgrounds of those to whom they minister.

Hudson draws upon the best of black theological principles for ministering in urban contexts in both traditional and nontraditional ways. In seeking to be relevant, Hudson emphasizes holy hip-hop as a culturally dynamic way of communicating with many urbanites, especially among the youth. Christians may not be all that aware of hip-hop music and the multifaceted culture associated with it. In fact, they may consider it bizarre to call hip-hop holy. But such a conclusion would suffer from the same kind of ignorance and misassociations that prevent Christians and churches from benefiting from Black Theology.

Although Christians may at times struggle with being culturally relevant, Hudson guides us with regard to how hip-hop music and culture may constructively contribute to our proclamation of the gospel of Jesus Christ, and to our establishment of a godly lifestyle complementary to both scripture and hip-hop. For example, Hudson talks about the inner-city context of biblical writings, in both the Old and New Testaments. Both Habakkuk and Job address life in cities, and they talk about the oppression and suffering people experience—physically as well as spiritually. They also talk about the deliverance that God wants to provide people, liberating them from physical oppression as well as spiritual oppression.

The New Testament also embodies and instructs us with regard to ministering in a racially, ethnically, culturally, linguistically, and nationally diverse context, including urban contexts. Jesus was multi-lingual, and he ministered to more than Jews, even though he spent most of his time among them. At the end of his life, Jesus sent his followers out among all nations and all people groups in order to make disciples (Matthew 28:19–20). The book of Acts attests to the challenges his followers faced in making disciples of Gentiles, composed of different races, ethnicities, cultures, and languages.

In ministering to urban men, women, and youth, Hudson draws upon Cone, Martin Luther King, Jr., and other racially and ethnically diverse Christian leaders both in socially analyzing the plight of urbanites and in ministering to them, physically and spiritually. For example, black and brown youth suffer especially from racist practices, unjustly leading to inequality in their education, employment, and mass incarceration. In response, Hudson asks how Christians and churches may effectively minister to such youth. Customary calls for prayer and compassion represent a partial answer, but scripture and Christian civil rights leaders also call for advocacy on behalf of the physical impoverishment that people experience as well as for their spiritual impoverishment.

If ministry to urban people today—including black and brown youth—is to be biblical and effective, then there needs to occur greater advocacy on behalf of their physical wellbeing. Just as Jesus advocated on behalf of the poor, the blind, the oppressed, and those held captive, Christians and churches today need to advocate for others individually, socially, and politically (Luke 4:16-30). Such advocacy is not easy, and it is often criticized by Christians as well as non-Christians. Yet, if Jesus' gospel is to be embodied as well as proclaimed today, then Christians and churches need to be bold in acting counter-culturally—countering individual sins, social sins, and political sins. By the grace of God, through the presence and power of the Holy Spirit, ministry can become more successful, even in the complexity of inner-cities with all its rich diversity.

Hudson knows about the city, about ministry to black and brown youth, and about how hip-hop serves as a bridge for communicating with, ministering to, and empowering them. He is not the only Christian to emphasize the holy use of hip-hop for ministry, but more people need to follow Hudson's guidance if they want to become more empathetic and effective in ministering to inner-city youth. Of course, he talks about the theological and existential challenges of holy hip-hop, but Hudson considers ignorance of (through intentionally ignoring) it far more disastrous than intentionally implementing hip-hop music and culture for urban ministries. Given the extreme challenges today involved with ministering to black and brown youth in inner-city contexts,

Hudson gives us creative insight into how Christians and churches may become more effective in ministering to them.

**Don Thorsen, PhD**, is Professor of Theology, and Chair of the Department of Theology and Ethics, in the Azusa Pacific Seminary at Azusa Pacific University, located in Azusa, California.

# Preface

THE FOCUS OF THIS work is not to alienate or cause the number of individuals who may read it to shun it as the work of a pastoral heretic who is displeased with the social order, rather than with the theological work of the church. The readers which this work targets, for any number of reasons, understand and appreciate the gravity of its contents as it applies to inner-city ministry as examined through the eyes of its youth—black and brown.[1] There will be agreement, disagreement, criticism, and rejection of its ideological polemic from the academic, theological, and social communities. In a work by Tim Wise, *Dear White America*, he states,

> Such is the nature of ideological polemic. It tends to find readership amongst those already predisposed to agreement with the bulk of its contents, thereby missing the vast throngs of others who could perhaps benefit from those contents but will studiously avoid them precisely because they can tell—perhaps from the title or the jacket blurbs, or because they are already familiar with the author—that they won't likely agree with much of what lies inside.[2]

---

1. By way of definition in this work, *black is a socially based racial classification related to being African American, with a family history associated with institutional slavery. The term brown is used to mean a particular racial identity non-white Amerindian-descended Hispanic and Latino American communities in an American context.*

2. Wise, *Dear White America*, 9.

This work is intended as an unpretentious account of complex crises as experienced among our black and brown youth at large, and black and brown youth in the inner-city in particular. This work is less about people and more about institutions—the dichotomy of the institution of the church and the social institution of systems that effect a theological mindset.

The double-edged sword of Black Theology and Holy Hip-hop will cut a new faith in inner-city ministry that will initiate freedom against personal pain and systemic oppression and free minds from self-hate and submissive control. Inner-city faith needs a mixing of the militancy of an X (Malcolm) added to the hope of a King (Martin Luther King Jr.). This work will challenge leaders to abandon their traditional aims at preserving and reviving the substance of their respective traditions, and as with Jesus Christ, risk alienation from their particular communities for the passion of His people.

# Introduction

OVER THE PAST SEVERAL years of theological study, there are two areas of black culture that have generated both a conflict and challenge to Christian tradition: Black Theology and Holy Hip-hop. As a pastor, mentor, and educator, I struggle with how to bring redemption and spiritual formation to the inner city poor, young black and brown youth in particular. Throughout my pastoral career, I have been involved with young people and their families, and have seen the agony of life in the ghetto as people struggle to hold on to their faith in God, while simultaneously surviving in conditions hostile to that faith. Although we learn from a variety of theologies, Holy Hip-hop and Black Theology are crucial for inner-city spirituality among its black and brown youth. No other discourse seems to be as effective for addressing their needs. Therefore, the goal of this book is to solidify the relationship of Black Theology and Holy Hip-hop.

To better understand a definition of Black Theology as utilized in this study, a concept developed by James Cone will become the foundation for consideration. Cone says:

> Black Theology is a theology of black liberation. It seeks to plumb the black condition in the light of God's revelation in Jesus Christ, so that the black community can see that the gospel is commensurate with the achievement of black humanity. Black Theology is a theology of "blackness." It is the affirmation of black humanity that emancipates black people from white racism, thus providing authentic freedom for both white and black people. It

affirms the humanity of white people in that it says "No" to the encroachment of white oppression.[3]

Black Theology must draw upon the scriptures to construct a social gospel that makes God central to both those who speak the language of the streets and the language of the church. Simultaneously understanding that Holy Hip-hop is a countercultural, subversive vehicle through which disaffected black and brown youth can engage the resources of biblical faith and Christian tradition. Black Theology flows from black thought and differs from American white theology in that it (American white theological thought) defines the theological task independently of black suffering. Christianity has been compatible with white racism, and the appearance of Black Theology on the American scene is due primarily to the failure of white religionists to relate the gospel of Jesus to the pain of being black. Cone argues black religious thought and Black Theology together share a simple reality: an indestructible belief in freedom, a freedom born in the African environment that includes aspects of black life and culture.

This book will describe the spiritual features of Holy Hip-hop, explore its themes and practices, expose its history and theology, and identify its goals and objectives. This will involve an analysis of the lives of the hip-hop generation in the inner-city and the complex social problems and negative factors that affect their lives and hinder their spiritual formation. I will examine claims that the Holy Hip-hop movement equips and inspires young people to surmount their problems and the negative aspects of their environment in order to create a more stable life for themselves.

Hip-hop has been both an empowering and debilitating phenomenon for black and brown youth culture. Hip-hop is empowering because it creates a sense of pride, resistance, and victory in the face of adversity. Hip-hop embraces a style in fashion, language, attitude, and business. It opened the creative doors for its members to express their inner-most feelings. Hip-hop gives its generation a voice and a sense of community. Conversely, hip-hop

3. Cone, *A Black Theology of Liberation: Twentieth Anniversary Edition*, 152.

is debilitating because it reinforces the stereotypical and negative images of black and brown youth portrayed through the media. It affirms youth who stand on the street corners with their pants sagging below their butts in a way that communicates shiftless, slothful men and women. It encourages men to imitate pimp rappers who brag about how many women (hoes) they have in different zip codes and their financial prowess at making money through selling drugs. Furthermore, it romanticizes criminal activities of black and brown youth who have adopted a lifestyle of chronic law-breaking. The effects of these negative, stereotypical images of black and brown youth defeat their potential and color them as social misfits.

So what is hip-hop? What is the difference between hip-hop and Holy Hip-hop? Holy Hip-hop is but one area of the "rap" genres; this genre is set aside (sanctified) for God. This is a very important point to this discussion; the main difference between hip-hop and Holy Hip-hop is that hip-hop makes no room for Christ; Holy Hip-hop makes only those rap lyrics that deal with Christ. Additionally, hip-hop in its original design, during the 1970s, was designed for healing, restoration, and communication. It was a common vehicle for black and brown young adults to come together. . . not apart.

Socially, hip-hop has been attributed as a "black" movement. For many people, pastors included, the word "hip-hop" produces some of the most negative, vile perceptions of young black and brown youth. . . God's babies. For these people, the word "hip-hop" suggests music that contains cursing and music videos that depict graphic sexual behavior, violence, gangs, drugs, an unabridged focus on money, cars, oversized rims, jewelry, saggy pants, and tattoos. For them, hip-hop suggests a culture gone wrong; a culture absent of God and the moral character that emulates evil rather than holiness; a culture not able to be redeemed. But this is not hip-hop; this is not what God intended for this culture.

In most cases, hip-hop and all the negative connotations associated with it are, in fact, reflections of an American reaction to issues that have always been a problem with youth, no matter what generation it happens to affect. These issues continue to plague generations of young people as they grow into adulthood and leave unresolved, fragmented emotions that hinder them from productive maturity. These issues include racism, violence, drugs, alcohol, loneliness, inadequate education, abandonment, lack of security, finance, self-esteem, broken homes, and families. It is the negative implications of hip-hop that have consistently impacted the growth of this culture within the church. Furthermore, millionaire rappers are seen in their expensive cars and homes signifying the reality of the "American Dream" come true through the "American Nightmare" of those (their fan base) struggling in the ghettos. The gangsta rap music industry valorizes the very conditions which young black and brown youth wish to escape. But the lure of money, fame, and fortune is irresistible in the context of poverty.

It is my hope that this book will better equip pastors to bring a new method of teaching and ministering to this generation. It is my hope that as pastors and leaders in the Body of Christ that we free youth from the social handcuffs of arrested spiritual development. Moses turned over the mantle to Joshua; Elijah turned over the mantel to Elisha; and Saul had to give it up to David, and David to Solomon. The pattern is that the church, as the Body of Christ, must continue to turn over the mantle. The church, as the Body of Christ, must continue to grow and prosper. Our youth must continue to see the love of Christ in the church as the church continues to see the future in them. Theology cannot allow the church to continue to get older as the streets continue to get younger.

# BIBLICAL INTERPRETATIONS

# Habakkuk: "I Have a Dream"

THE HUMAN EXPERIENCE OF wickedness, deceit, crime, mistrust, racism, and other social pathologies make people doubt the reality of God. It at least makes people doubt that God will intervene to defeat evil. Doubt is exacerbated when evil appears to prosper in spite of God's providence and sovereignty. Faith and prayer do not seem to work. Patience is lost with God's promises of liberty and freedom. Throughout history, men and women have asked the question, "Why?" It is a natural question that demands a supernatural answer. Believers and non-believers have asked this common question in a quest for a simple theological understanding of human tragedy and injustice.

In an effort to draw out a biblical perspective upon the human struggle, especially as that struggle takes shape in the inner-city, this study will engage with two biblical narratives: Habakkuk and Job. The questions presupposed and asked by Habakkuk have been asked by God-fearers throughout generations. Even as prayers become desperate, the point must be clearly made that God is not accountable to man (Hab 2:1–5).[1] Francis I. Andersen states, "The two realities—God and the world—do not seem to fit. The task of making them fit is daunting. Biblical faith holds on tenaciously to both realities. The world is real; the God who made it is also real. This is what Habakkuk believes. He manages somehow to survive by faith" (Hab 2:4b).[2]

---

1. All scriptural references will come from the King James translation.
2. Andersen, *Habakkuk*, 11.

Finally, this chapter is concerned with two key concepts in relationship to God and the inner-city experience: trust and faith. From our engagement with Habakkuk and Job, a clear inner-city perspective on trust and faith in God will emerge. Do the questions asked of God show lack of faith and trust? Is the inner-city undergoing a temporary trial like the people of God in the vision of Habakkuk or is it experiencing demonic attack and punishment like Job? The answers to these questions (or at least an attempt to understand the nature of the questions) will determine how Black Theology can assist in the space between the question and God's answer; because in that space is a test of our faith.

Biblical scripture reveals that at least two men "wrestled" with God's divine plan. The book of Genesis reveals that Jacob, later to be renamed Israel, wrestles with a theophanic being until his blessings were realized (along with a broken hip). But another biblical account of a man who "struggles" or "wrestles" with God's divine plan is Habakkuk. His name means "embracer" or "wrestler" and it is his answer to the question "where is God?" that is intriguing. Richard W. De Haan makes reference to other questions raised in this biblical account:

> Habakkuk was not a self-centered person concerned only with the comfort and safety of himself and his family. As a true patriot, he was deeply distressed by the moral and spiritual conditions about him. He loved his nation, and knew it was moving ever closer to the precipice of destruction by continuing to break the laws of God. Therefore, two anguished questions burst forth from his lips: How long? And Why?[3]

The theme of this three chapter book is "The righteous live by faith," and as one of the minor prophets of Judah, Habakkuk was burdened with a vision of impending destruction. The prophet struggled with God's apparent non-response to the injustices and violence which surrounded him. Chapter one contains the questions and complaints of the prophet (Hab 1:1 through

3. DeHaan, "Song in the Night," quoted in MacDonald, *Believer's Bible Commentary*, 1141.

1:17). Within these verses, Habakkuk asks his first question; "How long shall I cry (Hab. 1:2)?" After God answers this question later in chapter one, Habakkuk asked his second question: "Why (Hab.1:13)?" Although God speaks to Habakkuk prior to chapter two, His full reply is not yet received by Habakkuk until he stands upon the tower as a watchman and is quiet as he begins to listen to the voice of God. (Hab. 2:1—2:20). Lastly, chapter three reflects a prayer psalm that is intended to be played with a string accompaniment. Although it is not a part of the verbal interaction between God and Habakkuk as in chapters one and two, it harmonizes with those chapters because it expresses a strong faith in God in spite of deplorable social injustices and violence.

Much in Habakkuk can be applied to present day social conditions in the inner-city. The story of this prophet's wrestling with the question of "where is God?" in the midst of social injustice and violence seems appropriate within an inner-city context. Other questions generated by the continued frustration of God's people are also applicable: How long? Why? The Chaldeans can be envisaged as the oppressive institutions that protect, and in many cases, produce the violence, iniquity, and injustices against God's inner-city peoples; that is, the justice system, political system, and even religious systems within the church. All these oppressive systems add to the chaotic conditions found in the inner-city. Hiebert states:

> Habakkuk's central concern for justice places him solidly in the tradition of Israel's prophets. Like his predecessor Isaiah and his contemporary Jeremiah, Habakkuk calls attention to and criticizes the miscarriage of justice in the political, judicial, and economic institutions of Judah and of its capital, Jerusalem. Also in the tradition of Israel's prophets, he predicts the demise of this unjust society as a result of coming events in which God will punish its unjust leaders and reestablish equity and proper order.[4]

Chapter 1:4 seems to anticipate our criminal justice system. Habakkuk was concerned that the law had slacked off. Even today

4. Hiebert, *Habakkuk*, 623.

in our court systems the scales of justice are unfairly balanced. Many in the inner-city view American justice as a blindfolded concubine that lifts the covering from one of her eyes to wink favor upon the elite and tip the balance of equality toward those who can pay her price. Hiebert goes on to explain that:

> The words "strife" and "contention" derive from the legal sphere of Judean society. They appear to describe stresses in Judah's judicial system brought on by irresponsible litigation or the failure to administer justice properly. Even Habakkuk's use of the term "righteous" for the victims of such abusive policies may identify them as society's poor and marginalized. Such abuses of power are ultimately to blame, according to Habakkuk, for a society in which justice is absent and the law ineffectual."[5]

In the days of Habakkuk, as of today, the violence and injustice that was pervasive and perpetrated upon poor people was a public spectacle. Both the wicked and the righteous witnessed the chaos. Who then is taking up the fight for the abused and underprivileged? Since God will do nothing without first revealing it to his prophets, why have the prophets not yet spoken? When the heart and mind are corrupted by the circumstances (in this case iniquities) that are prevalent in the environment, the imitation of the wicked becomes an accepted practice, a choice to act like everyone else in that environment. More especially, when it appears that God is secretly helping the wicked by prospering them without reproach, it shatters the faith of the righteous and moves them to seek this favor in the same unrighteous way. Habakkuk had to endure seeing God's chosen people act like the heathens around them.

The small three chapter book of Habakkuk bears witness to three phrases in our relationship with God: the feeling of abandonment, remembrance of what God has already done, and thanksgiving/praise. Habakkuk cycles us through all three phrases en route to an understanding of God's plan. First, when God does not change earthly circumstances in response to questioning and

5. Ibid., 631.

complaints, it makes us feel like God does not see us, and if He does see us, why does He not do something about our circumstances? This question of "why?" becomes a vexing presence. Without God's immediate response to our first question, the second question becomes, "how long?" Furthermore, in the midst of our impatience with the slow response of God, the final question becomes, "where is God?" Surely God is present in the midst of these oppressive iniquities. Why does God not intervene on behalf of His children? It is hard to see how this period of questioning can still be part of God's plan, because the questions themselves rise out of a loss of faith. When it appears that God is allowing wickedness to reign, injustice to flourish, and inequality to manifest itself in the lives of oppressed people, it does not seem that God has any plan at all. But the message of Habakkuk is that God nevertheless does have a plan. Second, in this cycle of understanding God's plan, it becomes necessary to remember what God has already done. This part of the cycle does not usually happen until the soul has exhausted itself in complaining and questioning and God takes advantage of that moment to graciously answer impatient supplications with a reminder of His acts.

Third, thanksgiving and praise must be rendered to God in preparation for God's response in whatever way God chooses to respond. The questions are then put in their proper perspective; and believers fulfill the callings to which God has summoned them. As Habakkuk had to fulfill his calling as a watchman and intercessor, so believers must fulfill their callings as the way of assuming their place in the plan of God. Praise and thanksgiving propels believers to their place in God's plan. Ralph Smith speaks of Habakkuk's attitude of praise:

> And while he waits for the ultimate victory, he says that he will rejoice and exult in the LORD even though there may not be any visible or external signs of his presence or favor. The words "rejoice" and "exult" each have the cohorative attached. This is the strongest possible way to say that one is determined to rejoice in the LORD regardless of what does or does not happen. Faith means

loving and serving God regardless of circumstances. For the just to live by faith means that he is to be faithful to God in his living.[6]

The application of Habakkuk's vision for Judah in comparison to the inner-city context is a demonstration that even though injustice and iniquities abound in the daily lives of believers, God does not overlook sin; He will deliver. Equally important, Habakkuk demonstrates that God will not allow wickedness to prosper. God's judgment was not only upon the nation He chose as the instrument of judgment, but also upon His people who were as corrupt, violent, and sinful as the chosen tool of judgment. However, the deliverance from both sin and judgment is available to God's people. Faith is the key to deliverance and the theme of the prophet. Even in the inner-city, the *just shall live by faith*.

---

6. Smith, *Micah-Malachi*, 117.

CHAPTER 2

# Job: Retribution versus Vindication

THE BOOK OF JOB is another account of a man who pondered the question, "where is God?" Like Habakkuk, Job was a man of God whose faith was tested. Habakkuk experienced injustice, iniquities, and violence as part of a nation. In contrast, Job endured an individualized, personalized oppression. Job's name means "the hated or persecuted one." Both Job and Habakkuk are valuable for this study because each book proclaims God's providence in the midst of suffering, and as such, each book rises to meet a theological challenge. They explain in their own way why God allows righteous people to suffer. Each book gives direct answers about those sufferings: God allows the righteous to suffer in order to expose their frailty and sinfulness while strengthening their faith and purifying them. The book of Job further shows that God is in complete control over Satan and therefore deserves complete trust. The message contained in Job has a practical, contemporary inner-city application.

Although the story of Job is one of individual suffering, the narrative still bears implications for the experience of suffering and oppression at a corporate or national level. "The silent sharing of suffering is a manifestation of fellowship."[1] The book of Job is ultimately a message for a fellowship. In the inner-city context, faith is confronted with key questions: How does God's love reveal liberation in a social construct characterized by poverty and oppression? What words are used to tell people who are just surviving that there is abundant life in God through Christ right now?

1. Gutierrez, *On Job*, 7.

9

"The innocence that Job vigorously claims for himself helps to understand the innocence of an oppressed and believing people amid the situation of suffering and death that has been forced upon it"[2] Examination of the main themes of Job will be scrutinized through the lens of the inner-city context and exploration of how those themes apply to social constructs that engender oppression and poverty in the inner-city will be discussed. The question how to relate to God in view of suffering of the innocent will be ask from Job's perspective.

In his study of Job, Gustavo Gutierrez articulates the difference between temporal retribution and disinterested religion. Temporal retribution, he argues, was a prevailing doctrine at the time the book of Job was written. It maintained that poverty was God-meted punishment for being sinful and lazy, while wealth was God's reward for honest and hard-working people. Riches and health on the one hand, poverty and sickness on the other are what God decrees, respectively, for those who live virtuously or un-righteously.[3] Disinterested religion, on the other hand, is the act of believing "for nothing," that is to say, expecting no rewards from God. Gutierrez explains only a faith and behavior of this kind can be offered to a God who loves freely and gratuitously. Drawing upon the perspectives of both Black Theology and disinterested religion the question arises, "How are we to talk about a God who is revealed as love in a situation characterized by poverty and oppression?"

There is a vested interest and stake in how to relate God to the brutal facts of suffering and oppression. It is important to assert, contrary to elitist scholarship with its pretensions of "neutrality" and "objectivity," that it is legitimate to bring these interests into conversation in an engagement with the biblical text. A Christian reading of Job that applies its message to the inner-city has legitimate cause to make suffering central in theological understanding. Theology in the inner-city is a dead enterprise if God is not opposed to suffering and oppression.

2. Ibid., xxiii.

3. Ibid., 22.

Gustavo Gutierrez's reflections on retributive theology vs. disinterested religion are applicable to our inner-city discussion. From an inner-city analogy, the man, Job, represents a collective process of inner-city black and brown experience and its relationship to a theology of God's involvement and participation in that experience. Gutierrez states, "The poor and the marginalized have a deep-rooted conviction that no one is interested in their lives and misfortunes. They also have the experience of receiving deceptive expressions of concern from persons who in the end only make their problems all the worse."[4] Furthermore, by way of analogy, Job's three friends represent "traditional church (theology)" that appears out of touch with the tragic chaos of the social conditions in the inner-city; that is, a wasted energy who vocalize reserved "excitement" about change but do not actually do anything. Emerson and Smith explain:

> Because evangelicals view their primary task as evangelism and discipleship, they avoid "rocking the boat," and live within the confines of the larger culture, but most typically their influence has been limited to alterations at the margins. So despite having the sub-cultural tools to call for radical changes in race relations, they most consistently call for changes in persons that leave the dominant social structure, institutions, and culture intact.[5]

Talking to God in the midst of human suffering is as difficult as *hearing* from God in human suffering. Gutierrez states, "The suffering of the innocent and the questions it leads them to ask are indeed key problems for theology—that is, for discourse about God. The theology of liberation tries to meet the challenge."[6] This language of liberation, this "talk" of suffering while loving, is the point of this discourse. There must be a more realistic "hands on" understanding of God for those who suffer in order to more effectively communicate with them. James Cone agrees and clarifies:

4. Ibid., 24.

5. Emerson and Smith, *Divided by Faith*, 21.

6. Gutierrez, *On Job*, xv.

> Black theology is a theology of liberation. It is a ratio-
> nal study of the being of God in light of the existential
> situation of an oppressed community, relating the forces
> of liberation to the essence of the gospel, which is Jesus
> Christ. This means that its sole reason for existence is
> to put into ordered speech the meaning of God's activ-
> ity in the world, so that the community of the oppressed
> will recognize that its inner thrust for liberation is not
> only *consistent with* the gospel but *is* the gospel of Jesus
> Christ.[7]

When the experience of injustice occurs, it provokes a feeling of hatred at the circumstances and anger toward God. Suffering and injustice naturally force the questions of why God permits wickedness and how God's love can be consistent with the existence of evil. The most universal question is, after all, "Why?" Gutierrez states, "The question for Job is not whether or not he is a sinner; the question rather is whether he deserves the torments he is suffering. We are confronted now with suffering that is unjust. As a result, the question "Why?" becomes even more heartrending and a source of even greater tension."[8]

Another question that challenges theological understanding in the midst of suffering and injustice is: Do the black and brown poor of the inner-city deserve what is happening to them? Scripture demonstrates that Job himself (who represents the collective process of inner-city black and brown experience and its relationship to a theology of God's involvement in that experience) did not believe he deserved what was happening to him, especially in response to the arguments presented by his friends (traditional church theology). Many black and brown poor of the inner-city do not believe that they deserve what is happening to them, but evidently there are a number of others who do believe this. Supporters of the doctrine of temporal retribution argue black and brown people within the inner-city are getting what they deserve because they are bad people, or because they are in some way inferior to

7. Cone, *A Black Theology of Liberation*, 1.

8. Gutierrez, *On Job*, 24-25.

their white oppressors. In fact, this type of thinking realizes no distinction between being bad and being inferior.

In classical form, Job's friends (traditional church theology), were teaching a theology that had no relevance to Job's situation, but they were convinced that their teaching was the definitive word on suffering and injustice. Furthermore, his friends chose to unearth fossilized teachings of the past, rather than consult living witnesses to how God leads in response to oppression and injustice. Gustavo Gutierrez states,

> The friends believe in their theology rather than in the God of their theology. The friends talk as they do because they have not experienced the abandonment, poverty, and pain that Job has. In other words, the dividing line is drawn by personal experience which these untouched theologians with their arguments do not know. Their encouragement is simply lip service; their words are useless and only increase the suffering of the hearer.[9]

The inner-city has been inundated with "lip service" of the conversion gospel narrative where oppressed people are encouraged to look "over yonder" for relief from oppressive and injustice conditions. Although traditional church theology has a voice, it is not a voice of a people who are seeking echoes of liberation from the mountain tops, but rather instead are no more than whispers of "we have always done it this way" from the depths of the valleys.

In terms of the argument presented by Gustavo Gutierrez, temporal retribution is not God's voice or his nature. As the book of Job concludes, Job's conversation with Elihu (Holy Hip-hop) leads to an understanding about how to talk about and to God. Elihu, who is considered a type of Christ in a Christian canonical view of the Job narrative, represents communication through Jesus the Messiah. Gutierrez asserts, "The revelation of God's plan when received with good judgment, will show Job that the doctrine of retribution is not the key to understanding the universe; this doctrine can give rise only to a commonplace relationship of self-interest with God and others. The reason for believing

9. Ibid., 29–30.

'for-nothing'—the theme set at the beginning of the book-is the free and gratuitous initiative taken by divine love."[10] The answer to the question "where is God?" is answered in God's speeches to Job. Wickedness and oppression must be defeated by God's people; that is, by an open-ended freedom of His creation to end oppression and injustice. Gutierrez states:

> The LORD is explaining that the wicked cannot simply be destroyed with a glance, God wants justice indeed, but God cannot impose it, for the nature of created beings must be respected. God's power is limited by human freedom; for with freedom God's justice would not be present within history. Furthermore, precisely because human beings are free, they have the power to change their course and be converted. The destruction of the wicked would put an end to that possibility.[11]

Gutierrez discovers three things that are apparent and applicable to inner-city questions about how to talk to God in the midst of suffering. Those three steps are, not just for Job (as a collective process of inner-city black and brown experience and its relationship to a theology of God's involvement in that experience), but also, by analogy, for the church. Gutierrez states, "There are three steps in response to Job: an acknowledgment that God has plans and that these are being carried out; a discovery of previously unrecognized aspects of reality; and a joyous encounter with the LORD. All this has an inevitable consequence: the abandonment of his attitude of complaint and sadness."[12] The argument must therefore be that the church must take the lead in being the voice of the oppressed and suffering. This voice, when spoken within the inner-city, must be voiced with the determination and compassion of Black Theology; an awakening of the black experience in the realization of God's plan. Evil never wins! Martin Luther King, Jr., aptly and prophetically warned the church of dire consequences if the divine summons to recover its purpose goes unheeded:

10. Ibid., 71.

11. Ibid., 77.

12. Ibid., 83.

If the church does not recapture its prophetic zeal, it will become an irrelevant social club without moral or spiritual authority. If the church does not participate actively in the struggle for peace and for economic and racial justice, it will forfeit the loyalty of millions and cause men everywhere to say that it has atrophied its will. But if the church will free itself from the shackles of a deadening status quo, and recovering its great historic mission, will speak an act fearlessly and insistently in terms of justice and peace, it will enkindle the imagination of mankind and fire the souls of men imbuing them with a glowing and ardent love for truth, justice, and peace.[13]

13. King, *Strength to Love*, 59.

# HISTORICAL INTERPRETATIONS

# CHAPTER 3

# A Critical Examination of James Cone's *The Cross and the Lynching Tree*

AMERICAN HISTORY RECORDS THE beginning of slavery as early as the 17th century. After 1619, Africans appeared in the colonies of Jamestown, Virginia and although historians do not give an accurate number, they estimated that 6 to 7 million slaves were imported from Africa to America. Many of those brought over from Africa were considered some of its healthiest and ablest men and women. It can be reasonably stated that America was already a slave (that is, to British rule) even before it perpetuated the same type of slavery on Africans; America and slavery developed side by side.

After the American Revolution, a newly developed constitution declared that slaves were only three-fifths of a person (property) and all but guaranteed the institution of slavery in America. Set to work in the tobacco and rice fields (and later in the cotton fields), African slaves were an essential and valuable work force to the economic development of America. Abraham Lincoln's views on slavery became quite evident in some of his speeches. In a speech at Peoria, Illinois in October 16, 1854, he stated:

> This declared indifference, but, as I must think, convert, real zeal, for the spread of slavery, I cannot but hate. I hate it because of the monstrous injustice of slavery itself. I hate it because it deprives our republican example of its just influence in the world, enables the enemies of free institutions with plausibility to taunt us as hypocrites, causes the real friends of freedom to doubt our

sincerity, and especially because it forces so many good men among ourselves into an open war with the very fundamental principles of civil liberty, criticizing the Declaration of Independence, and insisting that there is no right principle of action but self-interest.[1]

Theologically, this accommodation of slavery is documented and presents a greater challenge to the church. "Evangelicals usually fail to challenge the system not just out of concern for evangelism, but also because they support the American system and enjoy its fruits and sometimes fail to evaluate whether the social system is consistent with their Christianity."[2] What are the challenges that lie ahead for the church with regard to the sin of racism, slavery, injustice, and inequality? What is the church's responsibility for reconciliation of the Cross of Christ and a history of a system that enslaved, killed, and persecuted believers of the power of that Cross? Is there some semblance of the death of Christ on the Cross and the lynching of black men, women, and children in American history?

As one contemplates Acts 10:39, it is hard to imagine that hanging from a tree, a curse, and Jesus Christ would have any association; however, the lynching of thousands of black people in the South can bring to mind the hanging of Jesus on the Cross. It has been documented by some scholars that the church and the federal government were surprisingly silent during this time. The complacency and apathetic position of these two powerful entities that could have arrested this atrocity actually condoned its action by their lack of involvement. Similarly, during the days of Christ, the cross was the penal system of the Jewish Temple leadership and the lost sheep of Israel to put people to a cross by crucifixion as a way of punishing anyone who they viewed an "outlaw" or trouble-maker.

Cone draws upon this association to illustrate that the death of hanging blacks during the Jim Crow era was much like the death by hanging of Christ on the Cross. The thesis of his work suggests

1. Basler, *The Collected Works of Abraham Lincoln*, 255.
2. Emerson and Smith, *Divided by Faith*, 22.

that until an association of the cross and the lynching tree is made, or an identification of Christ with a "re-crucified" black body hanging from a lynching tree, there can be no genuine understanding of Christian identity in America and no deliverance from the brutal legacy of slavery and white supremacy. This "identity" has an important role in reflecting on the life of Christ and the life of blacks in the inner-city; identity with a hanging Christ and hanging blacks. It reflects an important message of *solidarity* with the blood of Christ and the blood of those who were oppressed and abused at the hands of the "system." The most quintessential picture of Christ comes from experience and relationship. James Cone states:

> The cross and the lynching tree are separated by nearly 2,000 years. One is the universal symbol of Christian faith; the other is the quintessential symbol of black oppression in America. Though both are symbols of death, one represents a message of hope and salvation, while the other signifies the negation of that message by white supremacy.[3]

From the perspective of Cone, the cross and the lynching tree share typical histories with regard to the purpose for each. If a comparison is drawn from the context of their function, the symbolisms of each stand out with phenomenal clarity. Katie Grimes argues:

> In this resemblance, the cross and the lynching tree interpret one another, as the lynching tree can liberate the cross from the false pieties of well-meaning Christians while the cross can redeem the lynching tree, by bestowing upon lynched black bodies an eschatological meaning for their ultimate existence. It is important for Christians to understand what the cross means not only in the abstract, but also in their own socio-historical context, since this is the context in which they must be disciples. Thus the recognition of the connection between the cross and the lynching tree ought to serve not as the

---

3. Cone, *The Cross and the Lynching Tree*, xiii.

end point, but as the launching point for a completely re-configured understanding of discipleship.[4]

The image of Jesus and the experience of Jesus transcended the traditional images of Jesus beyond the lynching trees, beyond the black experience, and beyond the "over yonder" conversion gospel. Edward J. Blum and Paul Harvey argue from the profound perspective of this imagery:

> White Americans sanctified their disdain for Jewish and Catholic immigrants by crafting and globally distributing a blond-haired, blue-eyed, non-Semitic Jesus. Faith in and depictions of this new "Nordic" Christ symbolized white Americans' righteousness-and self-righteousness-as they took control of foreign peoples, lynched black men, and barred or discriminated against immigrants. Most black Americans of the age used white images of Jesus in their churches and homes, but a growing number now had the resources, space and autonomy to picture the savior beyond whiteness. These were the first expressions of what would later be called "black liberation theology." From Harlem, artists rejected the white Jesus images around them. They blackened him for the first time with paintings that portrayed him as a lynch victim and by telling new tales of the Son of God born in the American South, teaching racial harmony and economic justice, and then crucified for such southern heresies.[5]

According to James Cone, Edward Blum, Paul Harvey, and Albert Raboteau, the lynching era occurred from 1880 to 1940, during which nearly five thousand African Americans fell victim to this atrocity. The lynching tree and the cross was a paradoxical religious challenge to Christian theology; lynching created a crisis of faith. Blum and Harvey note that the head of the Colored Women's League, Mary Church Terrell, confided in her autobiography that lynching "came near upsetting my faith in the Christian religion." She could not comprehend "how a crime like that could

4. Grimes, "The Cross and the Lynching Tree," 1.
5. Blum and Harvey, *The Color of Christ*, 11.

be perpetrated in a Christian country, while thousands of Christians sinfully winked at it by making no protest loud enough to be heard or exerting any earnest effort to redress this terrible wrong.[6]

The religious challenge to Christian theology and the crises of faith of lynching produced anger, frustration, and lost hope in the souls of enslaved blacks. "Christ crucified manifested God's loving and liberating presence in the contradictions of black life that empowered them to believe that ultimately they would not be defeated by the "troubles of this world," no matter how great and painful their suffering."[7] However, Albert Raboteau argues a different observation when he states:

> To conclude, however, that religion distracted slaves from concern with this life and dissuaded them from action in the present is to distort the full story and to simplify the complex role of religious motivation in human behavior. It does not always follow that belief in a future state of happiness leads to acceptance of suffering in this world. It does not follow necessarily that a hope in a future when all wrongs will be righted leads to acquiescence to injustice in the present. Religion had different effects on the motivation and identity of different slaves and even dissimilar effects on the same slave at different times and in different circumstances. To describe slave religion as merely otherworldly is inaccurate.[8]

As a consequence, therefore, to accept one's place on *this* earth soon became a matter of self-acceptance or self-rejection. Once again, imagery was a key element in the transmission and/or confirmation of this inferiority or vulnerability. Blum and Harvey argue:

> The religious iconography of segregation leads blacks to disparage themselves and reason that if segregation was considered "normal," it was then "correct; if correct, then moral, then religious. To be considered valid as a

6. Ibid., 180.

7. Cone, *The Cross and the Lynching Tree*, 2.

8. Raboteau, *Slave Religion*, 318.

social system, segregation needed the divine to be white. God "is imaged as an elderly, benign white man." Angels "are blond and brunets." Satan "is viewed as being red with the glow of fire. But the imps, the messengers of the devil, are black." Doomed on earth to a fixed and unremitting status of inferiority, of which segregation is symbolic, and at the same time cut off from the hope that the Creator intended it otherwise, those who are thus victimized are stripped of all social protection. . . Under such circumstances, there is but a step from being despised to despising oneself.[9]

The challenge, therefore, as Cone presents it is this:

The sufferings of black people did not end with emancipation. The violence and oppression of white supremacy took different forms and employed different means to achieve the same end: the subjugation of black people. And Christian theology, for African Americans, maintained the same great challenge: to explain from the perspective of history and faith how life could be made meaningful in the face of death, how hope could remain alive in the world of Jim Crow segregation. These were the challenges that shaped black religious life in the United States.[10]

Cone was influenced by three important men as he studied the relationship of the Cross and the lynching tree: Reinhold Niebuhr, Martin Luther King Jr., and W. E. B. Du Bois. Reinhold Niebuhr was a widely influential theologian of the twentieth century. "Among white theologians he was particularly sensitive to the evils of racism and spoke and wrote on many occasions of the sufferings of African Americans. Few theologians of the twentieth century focused as much attention on the cross, one of the central themes of his work."[11]

To Niebuhr, justice and democracy was more at the center of Christian social ethics than love; justice was love approximated

9. Blum and Harvey, *The Color of Christ.*, 182.

10. Cone, *The Cross and the Lynching Tree*, 3.

11. Ibid., 32.

and democracy was a method of finding proximate solutions to insoluble problems. "Man's capacity for justice makes democracy possible; but man's inclination to injustice makes democracy necessary."[12] Inspired from others like Nietzsche (who coined the term "trans-valuation of values,") the heart of Niebuhr's perspective of the cross was repeated in many of his writings. Cone explains that, "For Niebuhr the revelation of God's transcendent love hidden in Jesus' suffering on the cross is not simply the 'keystone' of the Christian faith; it is the very key to history itself."[13]

Niebuhr, however, vacillated between two extremes: the urgency to eradicate the sin of racism, and the practice of gradualism and patience on the part of those being oppressed. Cone accounted for these contradictions as due partly to Niebuhr's inability to see injustice through the eyes of black people. For Cone, it seemed easy for Niebuhr to walk around in his own shoes, as a white man, but it took more empathic effort to step into the shoes of those black people and see the world through the eyes of African Americans. Furthermore, Cone was convinced that Niebuhr knew about the brutality of slavery, injustice, Jim Crow segregation, and lynching because Niebuhr was a pastor in Detroit. Niebuhr, as others, had "eyes to see" black suffering, but lacked the "heart to feel" even though essays, speeches, and political meetings have suffering as its subject.

The second person that influenced Cone was Martin Luther King Jr. The lament of Cone for Niebuhr's inconsistent commitment to the racial problem in America is reconciled in his perception of Martin Luther King Jr. who struggled to redeem the soul of America. In an ironic statement of what Martin Luther King Jr. learned from Reinhold Niebuhr, Cone recognizes that Niebuhr could have benefited from learning from Martin Luther King Jr., as well. "King could have opened Niebuhr's eyes to see the lynching tree as Jesus' cross in America."[14] Cone acknowledges King as one of America's greatest theologians, "But if the lynching tree is

12. Niebuhr, *The Children of the Light*, 118.

13. Cone, *The Cross and the Lynching Tree*, 35.

14. Ibid., 64.

America's cross and if the cross is the heart of the Christian gospel, perhaps Martin Luther King Jr., who endeavored to "take up his cross, and follow [Jesus]" (Mark 8:34) as did no other theologian in American history, has something to teach America about Jesus' cross."[15]

Convinced by the Emmett Till lynching, Cone expresses that this event was the beginning of the Civil Rights Movement in Mississippi. According to King, "The Till lynching is one of the most brutal and inhuman crimes in the twentieth century."[16] This lynching sparked a spirit in poor and oppressed black people who had little to no formal education in philosophy or political protocol, it was religion and faith that offered the only recourse—and the language to fight against segregation and lynching came in the voice of Martin Luther King Jr.

Cone draws a similarity of doctrine between King and Niebuhr. He argues, "Like Reinhold Niebuhr, King believed that the cross was the defining heart of the Christian faith. Like Reinhold Niebuhr, King believed that love in society is named justice."[17] Cone then argues the dissimilarity between King and Niebuhr as he alludes to the Black Theology of King that Niebuhr could not appreciate. In consideration for the Black Theology of King, Cone argues:

> In considering the subject of God and the problem of race in America, King reflected that God's love created blacks and whites and other human beings for each other in community (thesis). White supremacy was the sin that separated them in America and in much of the world (antithesis). God reconciled humanity through Jesus' cross, and thereby white supremacy could never have "the final and ultimate word" on human relationships (synthesis).[18]

15. Ibid.
16. King, "Pride versus Humility," 232.
17. Cone, *The Cross and the Lynching Tree*, 70-71.
18. Ibid.

Martin Luther King Jr. was no stranger to the realities of the lynching tree and death throughout his family life. Alberta King (Martin's mother) was shot and killed on June 30, 1974 by 23 year old Marcus Wayne Chenault (a black man) as she played the organ of the Ebenezer Baptist Church where Martin King Sr. was the pastor. What was Martin Luther King Jr.'s connection of the cross to the lynching tree? Certainly it can be understood that his life during the Civil Rights era connected him tragically to the lynching tree; however, more than the realization of the lynching tree was his profound identity with the cross. It can be argued by Cone and others that for King, the cross represented suffering and deadly violence. Furthermore, shaped by his reading of the bible and the black experience, an answer to black suffering and sacrifice.

Lastly, the literary passion and creative theological insight that shaped the artistic liberation theology of Cone was W. E. B. Du Bois. Du Bois prefigured the theological and Christological insights about the Black God and Black Christ in black liberation theology during the late 1960s and early 70."[19] It is clear that Du Bois was not a conventional Christian; however, Du Bois was able to cite the gospels verbatim and held a firm conviction of his theological understanding that Christ was indeed black. All his parables and poems, as Cone continues, have parallels with the stories about the iconoclastic Jesus in the gospels, a Jesus whose values disrupted the status quo because he showed solidarity with poor blacks.

Du Bois was disappointed with "white religion" and described it as an utter failure. Cone argues that Du Bois could not reconcile white Christianity with the gospels' portrayal of Jesus. Du Bois founded *The Crisis* in 1910 for the NAACP to keep the religious meaning of lynching before America. In that magazine, Du Bois argued his belief that the white Christ was not the biblical Christ:

> Yet Jesus Christ was a laborer and black men are laborers; He was poor and we are poor; He was despised of his fellow men and we are despised; He was persecuted and crucified, and we are mobbed and lynched. If Jesus

19. Ibid., 101.

Christ came to America He would associate with Negroes and Italians and working people; He would eat and
pray with them, and He would seldom see the interior of
the Cathedral of Saint John the Divine.[20]

Today, the media is responsible for creating images that document
human history and stimulating the imagination for future hopes;
unfortunately, many of those images are "photoshopped," stereotypic shadows of what truly exists. Yet, it should not require such a
leap of imagination to recognize the visual and symbolic overtones
between the cross and the lynching tree.

Cone argues, "When visual artists painted the image of Christ
on the cross and painted him black, they were also referencing
Christ as a lynched victim. Simply turning him from white to black
switched the visual signifiers, making him one with the body of
lynched black people in America."[21] Even today in contemporary
artistry, hip-hop artists are having the same revelation of a new
face of Jesus. These artists are trying to find a relational balance to
Jesus and His relationship to their struggle in today's society. Many
of these hip-hop artists have expressed the same frustration that
was prevalent during the Civil Rights era. "Unlike preachers and
theologians, artists and writers were not bound by the inherited,
static religious traditions of white supremacists. Black artists were
defined by their creative resistance against an oppressive status
quo. They were free to say anything that gave black people liberating visions of their humanity."[22]

Now, those same social pathologies are expressed in the music of rap and spoken word. Daniel White Hodge describes how
the hip-hop generation articulates their image of Jesus:

For many Hip Hoppers, such portraits of Jesus have
been used as tools in the church's attempt to control and
maintain status quo. So why would any true Hip Hopper
want to join a religion like that? Instead, many Hip Hoppers imagine a different Jesus: not some blonde-haired,

20. Du Bois, "The Church and the Negro," 290.
21. Ibid., 101.
22. Cone, *The Cross and the Lynching Tree*, 113.

blue-eyed, White embodiment of perfection but rather a Black Jesuz. Black Jesuz is multiracial.[23]

One of the major artists that illustrate this idea of exposure of oppressive factors upon the lynching trees of inner-city struggle was Tupac Shakur. Not noted for being a prophet, Hodge informs us that Tupac had the artistic interpretations of Christ and how he could be perceived through the eyes and experiences of those who struggle with cries of "Why me, Oh, LORD! What did I do to deserve this?" Even upon the cross one could hear the agonizing cry of Jesus, "My God, My God, why hast thou forsaken me?" (Mark 15:34):

> Tupac took Cone's idea a step further and talked about a Christ figure for the ghetto—a Christ who smoked weed, drank liquor and had compassion for the hood; a human link to deity. This image was connected back to his thug life message and carried a messianic message of hope, vision and blessings for the downtrodden and hurt that dwell in inner cities.[24]

Michael Dyson explores the dynamic prophetic voice of Tupac Shakur. Dyson argues that Tupac Shakur's theology squeezed the various vulnerabilities of black life into verse without smothering its defiant hope as his language, inflamed with love for the desperately poor, resounded with a strong and great effect on the social structure of America. The thesis of his work implies that Tupac did not just become a thug—he became a metaphysical thug; a thinking man's verbal outlaw, a troubled prophet who had risen to articulate a truth that people could not possibly live without. "Tupac operated with a thug's theodicy. He may be considered what I've called a hip-hop Jeremiah, an urban prophet crying out loud about the hurt that he constantly saw and sowed."[25] Yes, even Tupac had this vision of God. Dyson states:

23. Hodge, *The Soul of Hip-hop*, 126.

24. Ibid., 128.

25. Dyson, *Holler If You Hear Me*, 206.

The fearlessness, even recklessness, with which Tupac confronted death had a great deal to do with the death he witnessed and made records of, the mourning he did in its wake, and the God with whom he struggled to make sense of it all. There is a culture of death in pockets of hip-hop and in poor black communities that is alarming for its pervasiveness and tragic in the way it victimizes the young. The obsession with death has to do with the relentless murder and mayhem to which youth are exposed. Gang violence, drug wars, domestic abuse, social dislocation, and displace rage at poverty erupts in ghetto death.[26]

The gospel is the "good news," and to understand the "good news," Cone argues, "The cross is the most empowering symbol of God's loving solidarity with the "least of these," the unwanted in society who suffer daily from great injustices."[27] The dichotomy of the cross and the lynching tree has far reaching implications from the historical slave era to the present day society. Much of what is present today reflects what happened in the past. Racism, through the message of religion, is a sin that tries to transcend the pure gospel of Christ. King argues, "The church has a schism in its own soul that it must close. It will be one of the tragedies of Christian's history if future historians record that at the height of the twentieth century the church was one of the greatest bulwarks of white supremacy."[28]

Religion is a message of division and justification. It allows for division in the way that theology is perceived and justified in the way that theology is used. Reinhold Niebuhr has demonstrated that he could write and preach about the cross with profound theological imagination and say nothing of how the violence of white supremacy invalidated the faith of white churches. "In order to feel comfortable in the Christian faith, whites needed theologians

26. Hodge, *The Soul of Hip-hop*, 226.
27. Cone, *The Cross and the Lynching Tree*, 156.
28. King, *Strength to Love*, 105.

to interpret the gospel in a way that would not require them to acknowledge white supremacy as America's greatest sin."[29]

In America today, there may not be obvious "lynching trees" or blatant acts of overt discrimination/segregation, but the "lynching tree" still exists; Jim Crow still exists, and injustice still exists. Cone states this is the church's most vexing problem in how to define itself by the gospel of Jesus' Cross. "The lynching of black America is taking place in the criminal justice system where nearly one-third of black men between the ages of eighteen and twenty-eight are in prisons, jails, on parole, or waiting for their day in court."[30]

Where do the cross and the lynching tree intersect for Americans as history continues to move toward an eventual meeting with God? It is easy to understand that fear of the unknown can hinder faith, reconciliation, and healing. When it is understood that communication couched in the language of love repairs the breaches opened by racism, the cross and the lynching tree become cohesive forces for change. "The seeds of change are planted in the faith; racial reconciliation is God's imperative. Conversely, racial division, hostility, and inequality are the result of sin. Christians' work is to show God's power by reconciling divided people. For true racial reconciliation, then, believers of different races must "admit, submit, and commit."[31]

29. Cone, *The Cross and the Lynching Tree*, 159.
30. Ibid., 163.
31. Emerson and Smith, *Divided by Faith*, 18, 54.

CHAPTER 4

# The Willie Lynch Letter

*Dark Prophecy of the Black Family*
*"Peep da Game"*

A PROGRAM IS A plan of things that are done in order to achieve a specific result. Programs provide an order that when the plan is followed will always yield the same result. Most programs cannot be altered except by the initiation of another program. Different programs are set for different types of applications; a computer program, machines, aircraft, animals, and even people. There are two programs that illustrate how behavior can be psychologically "programmed" to produce a repeatable, predictable, physical behavior: (1) The experiment of Pavlov 1902 with salivating dogs, and (2) the Willie Lynch letter. Each of these represents what is called a "conditioned response," that is, training a person or animal to do something or to behave in a certain way in a particular situation. An understanding of the experiment by Pavlov will lead to a better comprehension as to an application to the Willie Lynch letter and how that conditioning has maintained a generational "slave mindset" on black people to this day.

The original purpose of Pavlov's experiment was to simply measure the salivation of a dog when presented with food (unconditioned stimulus); salivation was the unconditioned response to the unconditioned stimulus. However, Pavlov noticed something more powerful; any object or event which the dog learned to associate with food (such as the lab assistant) would trigger the same unconditioned response (salivating). Pavlov soon understood something important about learning. The dog had learned to associate food with the lab assistant (or more exactly, the white lab coat). He theorized that this must have been learned because at one point, the dog did not do it, but there came a point when it did, so the behavior had changed.

Thusly, this change in behavior must be the result of learning. Next Pavlov introduced a bell as his neutral stimulus. Whenever he gave food to the dog, he also rang a bell. After a number of times repeating this process, he tried the bell on its own without the food, but now the bell on its own caused an increase in the salivation (unconditioned response). The dog learned an association between the bell and the food and a new behavior had been learned (*or conditioned*). The neutral stimulus (bell) has become a conditioned stimulus. Pavlov termed a new law, "temporal contiguity" that states, if the time between the conditioned stimulus (bell) and the unconditioned stimulus (food) is too great, then learning will not occur. By way of definition:

Unconditioned stimulus = the object or event that produces a reflexive natural response.

Unconditioned response = a reaction to the unconditioned stimulus.

Neutral stimulus = a new stimulus that does not produce a response

Conditioned stimulus = once a neutral stimulus is associated with an unconditioned stimulus it becomes a conditioned stimulus.

Conditioned response = is the response to the conditioned stimulus.[1]

The history of the Willie Lynch letter has created much historical debate. Many historians believe that no such letter or speech existed; that it is only a myth. It is assumed that the speech was delivered by Willie Lynch on the bank of the James River in

1. Pavlov (1897-1902). "The Work of the Digestive Glands." See also *Lectures on Conditioned Reflexes; Selected Works.*

Virginia in about 1712. The purpose of the speech was in reply to an invitation to teach his methods to slave owners there. The term "lynching" is derived from his last name. The point of the letter was to psychologically suppress slaves for generations. Alvin Marrow states:

> Historically, a title had not up until recently been given to this system, nor had an individual been credited with the development and packaging of such a productive system until the discovery of Willie Lynch's Letter. Lynch and company somehow were able to conceptualize the very essence of slave making methods. The amazement of the matter is that after reading the letter two hundred and ninety years later, the spiritual drugs of division documented in the archives of this speech have held true exactly as Mr. Lynch stated. (The minimum test of time, in which this method if used would control the minds of the Negro Slave for at least 300 years). The second phase of the curse of Willie Lynch included the strong prediction that the utilization of his method would ensure the control of the Negro state of mind for at least an entire millennium (thousand) years.[2]

This examination does not seek to prove or disprove the validity of the letter; however, the contents of the letter will be considered in association with the conclusions developed by Pavlov.

The opening greeting of the Willie Lynch letter indicates the relationship of Jesus on the cross to the lynching of blacks on trees. In the greeting of the letter, Willie Lynch is quoted as saying, "While Rome used cords of wood as crosses for standing human bodies along its old highways in great numbers, and you are here using the tree and rope on occasion."[3] Cone referenced this Roman atrocity and compared its imagery to that of the lynching of slaves in the South:

> God must therefore know in a special way what poor blacks are suffering in America because God's Son was

2. Morrow, *Breaking the Curse of Willie Lynch*, 20.

3. Ibid., 9.

lynched in Jerusalem. Jesus and other subject people suffered punishment under the Roman Empire as blacks suffered in the United States. He was tortured and humiliated like blacks. What are we to make of the striking similarities between the brutality in Rome and cruelty in America? The crucifixion of Jesus by the Romans in Jerusalem and the lynching of blacks by whites in the United States are so amazingly similar that one wonders what blocks the American Christian imagination from seeing the connection.[4]

The Willie Lynch letter, besides the greeting and introduction, had four elements for conditioning:

1. Cardinal principles for making a Negro

2. The breaking process of the African Woman

3. The Negro Marriage Unit

4. Controlled language[5]

An examination of each of these elements will find commonality with Pavlov's experiment of conditioning and observations will be made to how those elements have continued to condition blacks to the present day.

This type of inquiry is not exclusive to this project; Alvin Morrow has also done a significant amount of research regarding the Willie Lynch letter and its implications for blacks today. Many of the arguments he asserts will be utilized in this section. "In truth, Black America as a nation still suffers largely due to the implementation of his plan, which at its essence revolves around the deprivation of our historical base."[6] The thesis of his work comes from his belief that blacks today need to redeem themselves from the psychosis produced by the plan of the Willie Lynch letter. Redemption from slavery does not end with judicial policies and constructions; redemption from slavery begins and ends in the

4. Cone, *The Cross and the Lynching Tree*, 31, 158.

5. Lynch, *The Making of a Slave*, 9–11.

6. Morrow, *Breaking the Curse of Willie Lynch*, 13.

minds of those who see themselves as slaves. "My sole intention for this publication is to help us break the repetitive cycle enforced by the psychological division instigated by the words, plans, conditioning, and abuse brought about by use of the methods devised by Willie Lynch and his council."[7]

Lynch was a British slave owner in the West Indies. Because of his success as a slave owner, he was invited to the colony of Virginia to teach his methods to slave owners there. The purpose of the letter also has four elements:

a. Generational psychic chaos

b. Internal conflict

c. War

d. Perpetual disunity among the black man and woman once held captive in North America[8]

Morrow also argues, "Notice how the instructions in the Willie Lynch letter are still being used in the common work place, religious circles, and the black home. Understanding the division of the black female and male is essential today, because these two halves are mandatory for the construction of a free spirited, righteous, and civilized society."[9]

The arguments of Morrow, Alexander, Cone, Wise, Kashif Malik Hassan-El, and Emerson and Smith, et al. will be highlighted. The point of this study is to establish a hypothesis: the plan of the Willie Lynch letter (whether the authenticity of the letter is founded or unfounded) continues to be a psychological phenomenon that needs to be seriously considered in discussions of oppression and how the current society chooses to eradicate the sources of that oppression. Secondly, the first release from that oppression is a psychological healing that is best understood and communicated through Black Theology.

7. Ibid., 11.

8. Ibid., 7.

9. Morrow, *Breaking the Curse of Willie Lynch*, 13–14.

To begin this study, Morrow asks the question, "What makes a person a slave?"

> A slave is a person under the manipulation or physi-
> cal confines of another brought about by brute force or
> carefully skilled trickery or deceit. A modern slave can
> easily be defined as a person that carries in his or her
> mind the old ideas, plans, and will of the old traditional
> slave maker, even though they are no longer physically
> detained.[10]

As Morrow has suggested, there is a difference between the old slave and a modern slave. The modern slave carries over the manipulations of the physical confines of "another" which include the physical abuse, trickery, and brute force from that "other;" it is essentially a continuation of the slave mindset. A new modern slave (old slave thinking) suggests a new Jim Crow type of control. For the next generation of youth who are coming into adulthood, there is an expectation that they should have better lives than those of the generation before them. A point of the Willie Lynch letter is a guarantee that this "plan," if done correctly, will last for 300 years. Willie Lynch in his letter states, "I have a full proof method for controlling your black slaves. I guarantee every one of you that, if installed correctly, it will control the slaves for at least 300 hundreds years." In order for this system to be effective and long lasting, it needs two components: A slave maker and a slave master.

For the most part, it would seem that the slave maker and the slave master are one in the same; however, Morrow and Alexander each disagree and make the following distinctions:

> The slave maker can be defined as a person who uses the
> barbaric tactics of torture, fear, beating, and murder by
> example alone, to obtain control. Secondly, a slave master
> is a person who has studied the spirit, soul, and psychol-
> ogy on a subject in order to master the internal operating
> principles that actually makes the person tick.[11]

10. Ibid., 17.
11. Ibid., 20.

To translate this definition to contemporary times and the definition of the modern slave, and in keeping with the envisaged inner-city context, three considerations are possible:

1. The slave maker is akin to the police
2. The slave master is akin to the judicial system
3. The plantation is prison

Alexander goes a little further to establish a connection of the judicial system to the slave maker, "The dirty little secret of policing is that the Supreme Court has actually granted the police license to discriminate. The Supreme Court has indicated that in policing, race can be used as a factor in discriminatory decision making."[12]

One of the characteristics of the Willie Lynch letter is the comparison made of black people to animals. This black animalization is characteristic of what people understand about blacks (along with other stereotypes). The Willie Lynch letter makes this comparison:

> What we do with horses is that we break them from one form of life to another; that is, we reduce them from the natural state in nature; whereas nature provides them with the natural capacity to take care of their needs and the needs of their offspring, we break that natural string of independence from them and thereby create a dependency state so that we may be able to get from them useful production of our business and pleasure.

This "animalization" of blacks had invaded the religious thought of early Christianity. "The pre-1700 views that black slaves were less than fully human, did not possess souls, and were incapable of learning, as well as simple indifference by white Christians all led to a lack of interest in proselytizing slaves."[13] Blacks were seen through the religious lens as heathens, that is, barbaric, savage, and without God. Wood argues that slavery was indeed an advan-

12. Ibid., 130.
13. Emerson and Smith. *Divided by Faith*, 22.

tageous institution: because the slaves were viewed as heathens, enslavement provided them "the opportunity to cast off their heathenism and embrace the Christian religion," with no concomitant change in temporal status.[14]

It was this "animalization" of blacks that spurred the initial reason for lynching and the fear that black men would "rape" white women. Cone states:

> Because of their threat to white womanhood, black men must be carefully watched and violently kept in their place, segregated and subordinated. "Race-mixing," mockingly called "mongrelization," [sic] was always translated to mean rape, and it was used as the primary justification for lynching. As Theodore Roosevelt said, "the greatest existing cause of lynching is the perpetration, especially by black men, of the hideous crime of rape—the most abominable in all the category of crimes, even worse than murder."[15]

To better understand this "mongrelization" or "animalization" as it applies to the inner-city context, Alexander and Wise have argued it from the perception of criminality. Alexander argues, "By the mid 1770's the system of bond labor had been thoroughly transformed into a racial caste system predicated on slavery. The degraded status of Africans was justified on the ground that Negros, like the Indians, was an uncivilized lesser race, perhaps even more lacking in intelligence and laudable human qualities than the red-skinned natives."[16]

## The Willie Lynch Letter on Black Unity

> I have outlined a number of differences among the slaves, and I take these differences and make them bigger. I use fear, distrust, and envy for control purposes. I

14. Woods, *Arrogance of Faith*, 36.
15. Cone, *The Cross and the Lynching Tree*, 7–8.
16. Alexander, *The New Jim Crow*, 25.

shall assure you that distrust is stronger than trust, and envy is stronger than adulation, respect or admiration. Don't forget you must pitch the old Black male vs. the young Black male, and the young Black male against the old Black male. You must use the dark skin slaves vs. the light skin slaves and the light skin slaves vs. the dark skin slaves. You must use the female vs. the male, and the male vs. the female. You must also have your white servants and overseers distrust all Blacks, but it is necessary that your slaves trust and depend on us. They must love, respect and trust only us.

The systematic construction of the Willie Lynch letter has a foundation of division and ignorance. "We must come to the agreement that at the foundation of the slave makers' thinking what was and still is the belief that the Negro male and female must remain divided and ignorant, in order that his system may function according to his plans, uninterrupted in an orderly fashion."[17] When the discussion of ignorance is raised, the subject becomes a matter of debate and further speculation as to the division among black people. Carter G. Woodson (writing in conjunction with the Willie Lynch letter) suggests the "highly educated" Negroes separate themselves from their own people because of *how* they were taught, not so much to the extent of *what* they were taught.

The difficulty is that the "educated Negro" is compelled to live and move among his own people who he has been taught to despise. As a rule, therefore, the "educated Negro" prefers to buy his food from a white grocer because he has been taught that the Negro is not clean. It does not matter how often a Negro washes his hands, then, he cannot clean them, and does not matter how often a white man uses his hands he cannot soil them. The "educated Negro" gets less and less pleasure out of the Negro church, not on account of its primitiveness and increasing corruption, but because of his preference for the seats of "righteousness" controlled by his oppressor.

17. Morrow, *Breaking the Curse of Willie Lynch*, 28.

This has been his education, and nothing else can be expected of him.[18]

In a study by renowned child psychologist and University of Chicago professor Margaret Beale Spencer, a pilot study was designed using a team of three psychologists to implement it. Commissioned by CNN, her team tested 133 children from schools that met very specific economic and demographic requirements. Spencer concludes:

> All kids on the one hand are exposed to the stereotypes. What's really significant here is that white children are learning or maintaining those stereotypes much more strongly than the African-American children. Therefore, while white youngsters are even more stereotypic in their responses concerning attitudes, beliefs and attitudes and preferences than the African-American children.[19]

The implication here suggests that African-American parents have a greater burden to help mediate the ambiguities of race and color for their children and what they experience. Conversely, white families do not have to engage on this level, and they may well spend more time on spelling, math, and reading because they do not have the extra task of reframing these negative messages that children get from society. To conclude her studies, Spencer makes the comment, "The study points to major trends but is not the definitive word on children and race. It does lead to conclude that even in 2010, we are still living in a society where dark things are devalued and white things are valued."[20]

Division can be examined in the form of classism in the inner-city demographic. American social structure is divided in three major areas: Upper Class, Middle Class and Lower Class. Each of these classes represents a misnomer of true representation based on income alone with no regard to the identity associated

18. Woodson and Lynch, *The Mis-Education of the Negro*, 6.

19. Recent research confirming that black children internalize negative images of blackness is from "Study: White and black children biased toward lighter skin," CNN.com (May 14, 2010).

20. Ibid.

with each level. It is important to understand that classification of Americans based on income debilitates the value they place on themselves and others and becomes an erroneous opinion of people outside the immediate social class. Additionally, not only does social class distinctions divide economically, but geographic isolation based on those economic stratifications become the foundation for a psychological pathology that labels an individual based on where they live. In other words, where one lives is what one becomes—environment determines viability of self-worth. Within the inner-city, the realization of self is identified in the worldview of environment and culture. Consequently, an internal view of theology is secondary to the perceived reality of division within the geographic boundaries of inner-city life. In other words, God is realized only as far as the eyes of faith can see, and if all the eyes of faith can see is poverty, crime, unemployment, inequality, and injustice, faith is an incongruous element to hopelessness.

## The Willie Lynch Letter on the Black Family

We breed two nigger males with two nigger females. Then, we take the nigger male away from them and keep them moving and working. Say one nigger female bears a nigger female and the other bears a nigger male; both nigger females—being without influence of the nigger male image, frozen with an independent psychology—will raise their offspring into reverse positions. The one with the female offspring will teach her to be like herself, independent and negotiable (we negotiate with her, through her, by her, negotiates her at will). The one with the nigger male offspring, she being frozen by subconscious fear for his life, will raise him to be mentally dependent and weak, but physically strong; in other words, body over mind. Now, in a few years when these two off springs become fertile for early reproduction, we will mate and breed them and continue the cycle. That is good, sound and long range comprehensive planning.

The black family is one of constant dichotomy and undergird. The dichotomy of the black family stems from male/female negative relationships formed prior to the marriage; in more cases then not in the childhood development phases. Morrow argues,

> What we see occurring between black males and females in relationships is a constant power struggle until the dominance of one individual over another is finally decided. In seventy-five percent of the cases the black man and woman usually end up cutting ties or dissolving the marriage. In other words, when the natural leader's senses are dulled to the point where self-guidance is no longer present; and he begins to follow the follower—organization or family soon deteriorates.[21]

Domestic violence in the inner-city is an on-going problem. The reasons for such violence vary on the people involved in the violence, however, statistics prove that black women are more likely than any other ethnicity to experience some type of domestic violence. Domestic violence is a consequence of a double-edged sword of powerlessness because men and women experience this inadequacy. Bakari Kitwana states, "The very same contempt that young Black men held for racist policing, high incarceration rates, and limited employment options was also directed at Black women, referring to Black women as bitches, gold diggers, hos, hood rats, chicken heads, pigeons, and so on."[22] Kitwana goes on to discuss this double-edged sword of self-hatred in the following manner. "Black women resent Black men due to the failure of Black men to compete and hence bring the race on equal footing with their white counterparts. Likewise, many young Black men resent Black women because of the success they've enjoyed in contrast to the overwhelming failure of Black men."[23]

"When black men were lynched, black women not only suffered the loss of their sons, husbands, brothers, uncles, nephews, and cousins but also endured public insults and economic hardship

21. Morrow, *Breaking the Curse of Willie Lynch,* 42–43.
22. Kitwana, *The Hip-Hop Generation,* 87.
23. Ibid., 107.

as they tried to carry on, to take care of their fatherless children in a patriarchal and racists society in which whites could lynch them or their children with impunity."[24]

*Morrow Argues a Plantation/Prison System:*

> Today there is no difference in the level of social climate in the black community when compared to the condition of the black man and woman on the plantation. On the plantation scene blacks produced for the slave master a new generation of labor, and were the forcibly separated based on the dis-empowering of the black male. The black male was mostly used as a breeding stud to the point where natural responsibility input was viewed as not needed, due to the fact her children had been taken and turned over to the present authorities as a result of an absent, dis-empowered, or un-productive black male. Today in America the same circumstances exist, but the only difference is that the setting is more decorated due to modern transportation, and the range of motion for the black slave is more broad.[25]

This aspect of the letter has direct connection to what Angela Davis and other scholars call the "industrial prison complex." This industrial prison complex is a type of plantation where cheap labor in the form of its prisoners (slaves) work for the slave master and all the profits go to build more prisons. Bakari Kitwana states:

> Corporations also capitalize on cheap prison labor. Federal and state prisons once restricted prison labor to services and products made for government and nonprofit agencies. However, in 1979, Congress created the Prison Industry Enhancement certification program (CPI), which gave private companies access to prison laborers. Mandatory minimum sentencing and state laws governing private industry's use of prison laborers have created a captive, non-unionized labor pool, where benefits, vacation time, unemployment compensation, minimum

24. Cone, *The Cross and the Lynching Tree,* 122–23.
25. Morrow, *Breaking the Curse of Willie Lynch,* 46.

wages, payroll and Social Security taxes, and even human rights and anti-sweatshop activists are non-issues.[26]

## The Willie Lynch Letter on Black Role Reversal

Understanding is the best thing. Therefore, we shall go deeper into this area of the subject matter concerning what we have produced here in this breaking process of the female nigger. We have reversed the relationship; in her natural uncivilized state, she would have a strong dependency on the uncivilized nigger male, and she would have a limited protective tendency toward her independent male offspring and would raise male off springs to be dependent like her. Nature had provided for this type of balance. We reversed nature by burning and pulling a civilized nigger apart and bullwhipping the other to the point of death, all in her presence. By her being left alone, unprotected, with the male image destroyed, the ordeal caused her to move from her psychologically dependent state to a frozen, independent state. In this frozen, psychological state of independence, she will raise her male and female offspring in reversed roles. For fear of the young male's life, she will psychologically train him to be mentally weak and dependent, but physically strong. Because she has become psychologically independent, she will train her female off springs to be psychologically independent. What have you got? You've got the nigger woman out front and the nigger man behind and scared. This is a perfect situation of sound sleep and economics.

### Morrow's argument on role reversal

Four hundred and forty-six years later the old mind of black slave and white master have not been altered. We often wonder why they have not based on this quote. Ask yourself a question: Why was the reversal of the roles

26. Kitwana, *The Hip-Hop Generation*, 73.

between black male and female such a necessary ingredient in gaining total control over black man and woman?
So much to the extent, that this perverted altering of the
natural roles between the man and woman would insure
the white slave master future control for many more generations to come.

"As Black women become more educated as a group, more
are deciding that they don't need to be in a marriage to survive
(although single-parent income still puts Black women at an economic disadvantage). Marriage, then, has not become an option;
Black women are increasingly opting out."[27] The best contemporary example of this quote anyone can see on television five days a
week. The Maury Povich show is a blatant illustration of this aspect
of the Willie Lynch letter. The cries of the show's host, "You are not
the father," or "You are the father!" further amplifies and undermines the integrity of black male and female relationship. When
the host shouts out that "You are not the father," it is an indication
to the audience (mostly white) that black women cannot be sure
who they are sleeping with. It puts integrity in the hypersexual
stigma that black women have so many sexual partners that they
cannot remember or can say with an assurance who has fathered
their off-spring. Additionally, it is a sad commentary on the inability or obstinacy of black men who choose to project a "pimp"
persona and in that way tries to prove his masculinity by claiming
as many bed partners as he can.

The converse cry of the host, "You are the father," is an indication to the audience and the world that black men stereotypically
have babies all over the place and share no responsibility in raising
or fathering their children. The latter part of the show focuses on
DNA testing to prove maternity, fraternity, or loyalty. The black
male/female relationship has become a source of entertainment
for the world to enjoy. The black man has now deteriorated his
masculinity from MAN to DNA. With the world as our stage,
blacks have turned over their integrity in the name of money and

27. Ibid., 109.

entertainment. They have become a source of provocative confirmation. Did Willie Lynch get it right?

"Black men resent Black women for bluntly calling them on their inadequacies. Adding to the tension, many hip-hop generation men resent young Black women because they believe that Black women are not penalized for being Black and therefore have it easier than Black men."[28] Additionally Kitwana sees what the media has accomplished in light of this part of the Willie Lynch letter, "What about expressions like 'baby Momma' and 'baby daddy?' The terms are used routinely by the hip-hop generation to signify individuals who share a baby together. However, the words simultaneously suggest something about the relationship; usually the absence of the child's other parent. Generally speaking, the term connotes that there is no relationship with the other parent."[29] And yet Kitwana exposes on another term black male and females use as an assault on themselves. "The use of the terms "nigga," "bitch," and "ho" by Black men and women to address one another has (regardless of class) permeated our colloquial language. And although defenders insist the "n" word is simply a term of endearment, which is often the case, just as often the context is derogatory."[30]

Daniel White Hodge and Imani Perry have each seen this aspect of the Willie Lynch letter in this generation. With regard to the old mind of the black slave, Hodge states:

> The Civil Rights generation tends to see the post-soul person as immoral, disrespectful, irreverent, and "secular." The post-soul person tends to view the Civil Rights generation person as old school, out of touch, hierarchal and extremely judgmental. This has caused much turmoil between the two personas and for ministers; it only deepens the misunderstanding when you add in the theology and religion.[31]

28. Ibid., 111.
29. Ibid., 115.
30. Ibid.
31. Hodge, The Soul of Hip-hop, 62.

Imani Perry states, "I argue that masculinity in hip hop reflects the desire to assert black male subjectivity, and that it sometimes does so at the expense of black female subjectivity and by subjugating women's bodies, while at other times it simply reveals the complexity of black male identity."[32] The old mind black slave and that relationship to the slave master was accomplished by language. The communication that went between the master and the old slave allowed for an understanding of what the master expected. When this link is established by whatever mechanism that may require, the communication becomes the "peculiar institution" whereby identity is established and new realities are realized.

## The Willie Lynch Letter on the Language of the Game

Crossbreeding completed, for further severance from their original beginning, we must completely annihilate the mother tongue of both the new nigger and the new mule, and institute a new language that involves the new life's work of both. You know language is a peculiar institution. It leads to the heart of a people. The more a foreigner knows about the language of another country the more he is able to move through all levels of that society. For example, if you take a slave, if you teach him all about your language, he will know all your secrets, and he is then no more a slave, for you can't fool him any longer, and being a fool is one of the basic ingredients of any incidents to the maintenance of slavery system. So you have to be careful in setting up the new language; for the slaves would soon be in your house, talking to you as "man to man" and that is death to our economic system.

32. Perry, *Prophets of the Hood*, 118.

## The Willie Lynch letter on race mixing

Crossbreeding niggers means taking so many drops of good white blood and putting them into as many nigger women as possible, varying the drops by the various tone that you want, and then letting them breed with each other until another circle of color appears as you desire. What this means is this: Put the niggers and the horse in a breeding pot, mix some asses and some good white blood and what do you get? You got a multiplicity of colors of ass backward, unusual niggers, running, tied to backward ass long-headed mules, the one productive of itself, the other sterile. (The one constant, the other dying, we keep the nigger constant for we may replace the mules for another tool) both mule and nigger tied to each other, neither knowing where the other came from and neither productive for itself, nor without each other.

### Morrow argument on the word "colored"

The meaning of the word colored means something totally opposite to what black people have traditionally been made to think. In reference to cross-breeding the word "colored" has a hormonal effect, which means having the nature of, and is derived from the Greek word *horme*, impulse. The significance beneath the surface of these definitions as they relate to the intention of the slave master to produce contaminating the black slave genetically with the inception of Euro-gentile's DNA on a bio-chemical level. Not only is the bio-engineering of different shades necessary to create a psychotic self-hate race war among the black slave population necessary during the days of physical bondage; but today is reinforced socially through de-segregation formally known as racial integration. This illusion is another aspect of century old control methods used by every Pharaoh throughout history, which is the intermingling of the emotions through alleged social gains from wanting the material benefits that come along with uniting and defending the economic kingdom of the oppressor.[33]

This cross-breeding, when read in the terms of the letter, expresses how Willie Lynch wanted to teach his disciples about how to keep the black race diluted and confused, and eliminates those who accept the mixture from those who fail to be "transformed." Those who get confused will not follow the pure blacks, but instead will have more of the characteristics of the master; therefore, although in black skin, will have the image and likeness of the master. Here is a kind of "misfit" that is neither black nor white, but conditioned to be whatever the master wants them to be. In the end, this cross-breeding leads to an abomination to both races.

Pavlov's experiment seems to touch on themes represented in the Willie Lynch letter. One of those themes is the longevity of the laws established in both. Pavlov's experiment will always produce the same results as an unchanging law; conversely, the Willie Lynch letter is guaranteed to have the same result for 300 years and beyond. As we examine the definitions established by Pavlov, those definitions can be applied to the Lynch letter and black people theologically. Consider the following definitions in light of Lynch and black slaves:

1. Unconditioned Stimulus = the object or event that produces a reflexive natural response is indicative of *God*. God is the single deity that is common to man whether that man is master or slave.

2. Unconditioned Response = A reaction to the unconditioned stimulus. Since God is the unconditioned stimulus and does not change, the response to the unconditioned stimulus is *worship*. While it is true that man is guilty of the kind of worship in which he responds to the unconditioned stimulus, which is God, the worship true or false is also a permanent reaction.

33. Perry, *Prophets of the Hood*, 74.

3. Neutral Stimulus = A new stimulus that does not produce a response. In this study, the Willie Lynch letter has been identified as the neutral stimulus.

4. Conditioned Stimulus = Once a neutral stimulus is associated with an unconditioned stimulus, it becomes a conditioned stimulus. This conditioned stimulus is *slavery*. As a result of the Willie Lynch letter, slavery became more sophisticated and psychological.

5. Conditioned Response = the response to the conditioned stimulus. Morrow and the other scholars have identified areas of black life that have changed (reacted) to the conditioned stimulus as a result of the neutral stimulus (Willie Lynch letter) that was introduced:

   a. Break down of black male/female relationships

   b. Break down of the black family

   c. Masculinization of the black female while emasculating the black male

   d. Robbery of language and culture of blacks

   e. Dependency

   f. Fear

   g. Perpetual psychological slavery

Pavlov's experiment confirms and validates the intended results of the Willie Lynch letter's prime motive: conditioning. Pavlov, although not a psychologist, gave the elementary elements of behavioral psychology a foundation upon which to begin. The classical conditioning conclusions of Pavlov's experiment did not seem to have any direct connection to the Willie Lynch letter, but has opened the door for the premise presented in this study.

What is the solution? Is there a way to break the curse of Willie Lynch? How can a person peep da game? "First of all to recognize (peep) means to admit knowledge of the fact, being certain of the identification of a person as being known to one.

In defining game, it is characterized as a scheme pursued in order to plot diversion, an act of un-willingness to take one's place in natural order and to manipulate competitively."[34] The first rule of any game is to know what game you are playing and know who your competition is. Blacks have been so long on defense it has been difficult to think offensively. Offensive thinking seems out of place and awkward. Morrow states, "Since we are dealing with the reality of Willie Lynch's generational curse on black life in North America, we must admit openly and honestly to ourselves the truth of this matter at every turn. In doing so we will not unknowingly run a game on ourselves."[35]

In this "game," just as it is on the street, men and women are players, but in this game there is need to call a time out, go to the side lines and re-strategize a new defense to take the ball and get on the offense. Morrow explains, "And in most cases the ball is always moving or is the object subject to being controlled. In this example the term ball shall be replaced with, and symbolized with energy, which can be termed as will. It seems the ball in any sport is the center focus of the rivaling competitors."[36] Next, according to Morrow, there are three things in life that everyone desires. These three things, according to Morrow, being a part of the human psyche automatically spill over into our daily relationships. But due to Willie Lynch's mind enslaving techniques, these three desires are magnified more largely in black male/black female relationships. These three tendencies are: Recognition, Control, and Security.[37] Although Morrow has not mentioned God as of yet, he does continue with this renewed strategy by stating:

> The three are inter-woven meaning that a person seeking security will seek control to the extent of his or her insecurity. Secondly, a person who wants control will seek recognition to the extent that they emotionally feel they lack respect. Under normal observation this is phrased,

34. Morrow, *Breaking the Curse of Willie Lynch*, 105.

35. Ibid.

36. Ibid., 106.

37. Ibid.

as seeking attention or competing for attention. It is the feminine aspect of the ego that is more inclined to seek domination under oppressive or unjust circumstances. Since the feminine is representative of the emotional half of man (not necessarily male) it is the first to suffer being subject to domination, abuse, and subornation in any relationship. Under these circumstances female instinct normally seeks to recognition or control to obtain security.[38]

Lastly, Morrow suggests that the original African concept involves an honest admission of the role of a man and a woman in proper balance putting the man in the leading position in his home.

Although there are many aspects of Morrow's argument that make sense, it is not a complete way to "peep da game" if in fact our peep does not include looking in the direction of God. It is not likely that traditional Christianity will take on the role of communicating new ways to combat the psychological effects of the Willie Lynch letter in an inner-city context. "Because black theology is the theology of black liberation, it must break with traditional theological speech when that speech softens the drive for black self-determination. When Jesus spoke of the gospel as new wine, it did not mean a total rejection of Judaism. What he meant was that the revolutionary message could be restricted to the possibilities available in the old structure."[39]

Additionally, it's time for the church to wake up; the black church in particular. "The black denominational churches seem to be content with things as they are, getting fat on the misery of their sisters and brothers. Black churches satisfy themselves with white solutions to earthly injustices. That is why persons interested in justice in this world so often scorn the black church, saying that it is nothing but a second-rate oppressor."[40] The Willie Lynch letter (real or not) will continue to be a blueprint for disaster of the black community and a dark prophecy for black families. It is obvious

38. Morrow, *Breaking the Curse of Willie Lynch*, 108.

39. Cone, *A Black Theology of Liberation*, 61.

40. Ibid., 134.

that the black community is following some kind of disorganized behavior that de-stabilizes the black family, black male/female relationships, and self-hatred. The black community passed the 300 year guarantee in 2012, but it appears that this community still has much to do. Michelle Alexander exposes the nature of mass incarceration in light of the Willie Lynch letter; Emerson and Smith reflects upon the racist attitudes that stem from the evangelical community. James Cone continues to make his observations on the short comings of traditional American Christianity and its non-involvement in the lives of oppressed people; therefore, Black Theology is the only other alternative to speak against that oppression with the passion of freedom. Daniel White Hodge, Imani Perry, Bakari Kitwana and others have expressed the need for hip-hop to be a part of this recovery.

The hope is to open the ecclesial eyes of the church in order that it might be about the Father's business. The evil written in the lines of the Willie Lynch letter cannot be of a divine and sovereign God, and therefore must be judged as sin. Cone argues, "Black Theology is practically the only remaining radical perspective linking the liberating essence of biblical faith and Trinitarian theology to a cultural and political strategy for fundamental social change."[41] In line with this discussion, hip-hop's challenge to the church is clearly spelled out, "Hip-hop addresses the crisis of urban America and begins to seek spiritual answers connected to Jesus, while challenging the institutionalized church and questioning the centralization of power in pastors to bring about a higher involvement with God."[42]

41. Ibid., 159.
42. Hodge, *The Soul of Hip-hop*, 73.

# Chapter 5

# Holy Hip-hop, Black Theology, and Ministry in the Inner-City

Although we learn from a variety of theologies, Black Theology is crucial for inner-city spirituality among its black youth because no other praxis seems sufficiently sophisticated to address the complexities of their cultural environment. Many young black and Hispanic men of this hip-hop generation are under the bondage of the criminal justice system in some capacity, either on probation, parole, or some other criminal supervision. Within the geographic context of the inner-city communities, imprisonment is more the "norm" than school or employment. Psychologists have long observed that when people feel hopelessly stigmatized, a powerful coping mechanism, often the only obvious path to self-esteem, is embracing one's stigmatized identity. "For those black youth who are constantly followed by the police and shamed by teachers, relatives, and strangers, embracing the stigma of criminality is an act of rebellion—an attempt to carve out a positive identity in a society that offers them little more than scorn, contempt, and constant surveillance."[1]

This hip-hop generation faces social barriers that were not present in the Civil Rights movement; therefore, an irrelevance or generation gap exists in conversation with them. These barriers include economic recession, racist policing, high incarceration rates, limited employment options, and sub-standard academic preparedness. This leads to a feeling of inadequacy, incompleteness,

1. Ibid., 171.

and the lack of an ability to be a man or woman that provides, protects, and leads. The flood of this inadequacy flows over into other relationships and translates itself into a self-hate for themselves and one another. This becomes a mindset of gangs: individual inadequacy seen through the lens of violence equates to group superiority. It is inadequacy that dictates the male/female dynamic of the inner-city. Domestic violence is a consequence of a double-edged sword of powerlessness because men and women experience this inadequacy.

As a society, we must ask ourselves, what are they supposed to do? What is the language to be used to heal and connect with their struggles? The words telling them "you are no good," "you will not amount to anything," and "you are wasting your lives" is not the correct rhetoric for transformation. Young black women repeat words from their suffering mothers by stating, "black men ain't shit" or "a black man is a dog" and even the classic line, "you just like your good for nothing daddy." There has to be another way in which ministry can be realized for this hip-hop generation. Both socially and theologically, a new rhetoric must be employed to communicate to this generation with words they understand and practice in their lives. How does the church minister to the level of the inadequacy experienced in the inner-city? How do we change the thought process which in turn will change the way they live? How can theory and practice be one in the same?

Black Theology flows from black thought; what a person thinks becomes what a person believes, and what they believe soon becomes what they do. What does the hip-hop generation think about religion? The methodology that has always been used to teach about God is not the way it must continue. If the black church continues to teach as it has always taught, then it is not new; it is habit. The bible teaches that old wine should not be put in new wine skins. Gayraud S. Wilmore is an ordained Presbyterian who participated in the first meetings of the ad hoc National Committee of Negro Churchman (1966). He was one of the first to chair the committee's theological commission and shaped its pioneering black theological direction. In an interview with Wilmore,

Dwight Hopkins wrote this excerpt quoting Wilmore on black religious thought:

> If we are going to talk about black theology, we really need to go back to the beginning and not assume that black theology began with the publication of Dr. Cone's book in 1969. But when we do that, we have to agree that we are not using theology in the strictly academic and technical sense. What we really might use better is the term black religious thought.[2]

In other words, according to Wilmore, black religious thought and Black Theology together share a simple reality: an indestructible belief in freedom, a freedom born in the African environment which includes aspects of black life and culture, which non-black scholars would call secular, non-Christian, and sometimes anti-Christian.

In order to communicate freedom, one would have to be enslaved under bondage. Traditional Christian rhetoric does not convey this freedom effectively; neither can it academically explain present day enslavement to the extent that black people experience it. Dwight Hopkins states:

> Black theology believes that the God of freedom has created African-Americans to be free—to reach their full humanity. Freedom comes when black poor folk, led by the African American church, live out their freedom because God helps them in their daily struggle against personal pain and collective oppression. This is what Martin Luther King Jr. taught, black theology. A liberation movement needs to free black minds from self-hate and subordination to white power. Malcolm X taught this lesson.[3]

Simply stated, today's faith needs a mixing of the militancy of an X (Malcolm) added to the hope of a King (Martin L. King Jr.)

Black Theology speaks to a hip-hop generation because it lends its rhetoric to youth who do not have the patience for the

2. Hopkins, *Introducing Black Theology of Liberation*, 67.
3. Ibid., 5.

standard method of theology. There is a weakness and slave un-
dercurrent in the "waiting for the promised land" mindset. The
first section of this study considers relevant scripture passages that
pertain to God's involvement and identifies how God feels about
the poor, oppressed, and disenfranchised people. These scriptures
justify how this hip-hop generation could see themselves in their
context through the lens of Black Theology. These principles
become conceptualized against the backdrop of the inner-city
context. There is meticulous attention paid to the shortcomings
of how traditional theology cannot be relevant enough to support
the spirituality needed for the youth of this hip-hop generation.

Ultimately, this is an examination of how the conjugality of
Holy Hip-hop and Black Theology gives character to a new way of
speaking of God in these times. Holy Hip-hop and Black Theology will answer the question of how the church overall and the
Black Church in particular should minister to hip-hop youth. The
lives of hip-hop youth are against social barriers their parents and
grandparents do not currently know how to respond effectively.
If the Black Church does not address this new dynamic, it is prophetically setting the atmosphere for more unrest in the city streets.
The times of the Civil Rights movement are still moving, and it is
moving through the lives of this generation, and the generations
to come. "*The Fire Next Time*" that James Baldwin predicted in
1963 is here. And what is being seen, as quiet as it's kept, is only a
glimpse of what awaits. . . "if we now, before it is too late, together,
Americans old and young, across race and gender, with criticism,
insight and concern, rise to the challenge."[4]

A direct reflection is needed upon the Emmett Tills, the Tra-
von Martins, and Michael Browns along with all the other young
unarmed black men killed before their times at the hands of the
New Jim Crow. The church must relive the dreams of the Martin
Luther King Jrs. and find comfort from the American nightmare
of the Malcolm X's. Black Theology must evangelize a new black
identity in a society that wants to oppress, suppress, and deny human rights of life, liberty, and the pursuit of happiness, and the

4. Kitwana, *The Hip-Hop Generation*, xxii.

liberty promised by Jesus Christ (2 Corinthians 3:17) and the Constitution of the United States. Black Theology, expressed through the medium of Holy Hip-hop, is a new rhetoric of freedom.

How valuable is black thought to religion? The bible has always experienced some rejection by black men in the inner-city because they conceive it as being a "White Man's Bible." Historically, there can be no dispute that Scripture became a "control" of black behavior, thought and the feeling of inferiority. Two reasons come to mind, "Slavery affected every area of Southern life. . .the "Southern way of life" was an important byproduct of slavery. Whites supported slavery because the "peculiar institution" sustained their most deeply held social and political values, particularly, an aristocratic style of life."[5] Fred K.C. Price states, "This is the reason, so many Blacks are ashamed of their ancestry; we have been subtly, and not so subtly, programmed to think little of ourselves. . .the source of this belief is the big lie of inferiority that the white power structure taught to Blacks and Whites alike to maintain its control over slaves."[6]

Cone argues that there is a black "survival" ingredient in Black Theology that can only be understood from the perspective of another black person. There are three elements that represent the state of the community: first, the tension between life and death focuses on physical survival in a hostile environment (the ghettos and barrios). Second, the identity crisis focused on survival as a person—not only of food and shelter, but also belonging to a community that remembers and understands the meaning of its past. Lastly, white social and political power—hoping that socially someday whites would not regard the color of their skin as the ultimate judge of character.[7]

By maintaining a generational slavery mindset, the choices made by young black men complicate their struggle to survive and remain free outside the prison system. In a vicious cycle of unemployment, sub-standard education, poverty, and crime that

5. Miller, *The Modern Church*, 136.

6. Price, *Race, Religion and Racism*, 175–79.

7. Cone, *A Black Theology of Liberation*, 10–15.

is out of control, along with a political agenda of 'genocide,' young black men make the same choices of their slavery forefathers. Cone argues:

> The struggle to survive in a white supremacist society was a full-time occupation for black people. But how to survive with one's dignity intact—that was the challenge. Black men seemed less able to navigate the complex relationship between survival and dignity in the violent patriarchal South. Just out of slavery, they wanted to be men, much like white males—providing economic support and physical protection for women and children— but they were not permitted to do so. As a result, black men tended either toward violence, which often placed them on lynching trees, or toward passivity, which led to the loss of dignity: few other options were available.[8]

Most young black men and women on the streets of the inner-city have the opinion that, if there has to be a choice between survival as a "punk," and death as a "gangsta," then the choice is obvious. There are as many young black men dead as a result of gang violence than there are in homes with families; how does the church evangelize, heal, and restore?

The rhetorical voice of the Civil Rights Movement falls upon deaf ears of this hip-hop generation. This generation feels that the Civil Rights Movement is a thing of the past with no relevant knowledge of the way things are today. The Civil Rights Movement is not dead, but asleep in the grave of complacency. Despite their apprehension that the Civil Rights Movement is in a state of antiquity, the black experience has not changed. The black experience is overcrowded ghettos, public housing, over policing of black males, guns, crime, gangs, poor education, unemployment, and drugs. Black Theology is how to make some sense of purposeful victory through this type of experience. James Cone remarks, "The black experience is catching the spirit of blackness and loving it. It is hearing black preachers speak of God's love in spite of the filthy ghetto, and black congregations responding 'Amen,' which means

---

8. Cone, *The Cross and the Lynching Tree*, 139.

that they realize that ghetto existence is not the result of divine degree but of white humanity."[9] The goal, therefore, is for Black Theology to recognize God's presence in the events that affect the black community. How is Black Theology to accomplish this revelation? Who will preach the gospel so that what is heard can be believed by those who have lost confidence in God?

Tupac is a prophet even though much of society sees him as a thug or gangsta. "The gangsta's God—or the thug's theology—is intimately linked to his beliefs about how society operates and who is in control. For many thugs, 'God is the great accomplice to a violent lifestyle.'"[10] Tupac Shakur was an outspoken advocate for young black men in hard ghetto living conditions. He took it upon himself to speak about those things that young black and brown men in the inner-city lived through; he was their preacher. Although his rap seemed to be filled with hate and violence, he also spoke of hope and love.

The rap of Tupac, associated with hate and violence of ghetto streets, amounted to nothing more than a resolute mindset of the gangsta to die rather than live. The sentiment on the street is that hell could be no worse than the hell in the hood right now. A young hip-hop rapper once stated, "I'm in hell's kitchen with an apron and a hairnet." Death seems like the only way "out" in this gangsta mindset. Dyson speaks of Tupac's encapsulation of this:

> It is precisely this combination of mourning death, seeking to kill, and desiring to die that makes Tupac perhaps the most powerful symbol of the multi-phrenia that divides the young black urban mind. By rhetorically embodying the person murdered, the person wanting to murder, and the person mourning a murder, Tupac captured a huge range of desperate black response to death's dominion.[11]

Traditional Christianity does not communicate with the power of deliverance and redemption. The language of the preacher is

9. Cone, *A Black Theology of Liberation*, 25.

10. Dyson, *Holler If You Hear Me*, 211.

11. Ibid., 229.

not what the experience may be on the street. The church experience is not a valid expression of this oppression, but rap settles
the mind and provides an avenue of expression absent in the Civil
Rights ideology. James Cone explains what black revolutionaries
see as the traditional church weakness, "Reacting to the ungodly
behavior of white churches and the timid, Uncle Tom approach of
black churches, many black militants have no time for God and
the deadly prattle about loving your enemies and turning the other
cheek."[12]

A new mindset demands a different form of rhetoric. This
new rhetoric must match the anger and intensity of its source:
the street. If they are to hear, they must be listening; otherwise,
faith cannot come (Rom 10:17). The passion of Jesus Christ must
be experienced in the passion of the language that speaks to the
black experience. Traditional Christianity has not spoken with
the passion necessary to quench the fiery darts of black suffering.
"Black Theology is survival theology, it must speak with a passion
consistent with the depths of the wounds of the oppressed. American theology identifies theology as a dispassionate analysis of 'the
tradition,' unrelated to the sufferings of the oppressed."[13] This new
hermeneutic must be preached with a combination of the tough-
ness of the serpent and the softness of the dove, a tough mind and
a tender heart that includes the militancy of Malcolm X and the
hope of Martin L. King, Jr.

The two extremes of liberation through song are as far apart
as the generation "gap." Although sung at different times, liberation songs have the same theme: freedom.

James Cone states, "Black slaves were left trying to carve out
a religious meaning for their lives with white Christianity. They ig-
nored white theology and went straight to stories on the Bible, in-
terpreting them as stories of God siding with little people just like
them. They identified God's liberation of the poor as the central

---

12. Cone, *A Black Theology of Liberation*, 57.

13. Ibid., 18.

message of the Bible, and they communicated this message in their songs and sermons."[14]

Conversely, Cornell West shapes how hip-hop follows the same theme of liberation in a rap style that is reminiscent of their ancestors. Cornell West states:

> Hip-hop artists, rap musicians are not just young people trying to make money. They are young people who are responding to a shattered community, constrained opportunities, and are falling back on one of the two major traditions forged by black folk in the fire of oppression—the musical tradition. The musical tradition that has helped black folk stay sane. Singing through the storm. It has helped sustain the black person's sense of self.[15]

Much of black culture and history is conveyed in art forms, whether music, poetry, prose, theater, or dance. Black culture is noted for its emotional and passionate expression in art when words seem to fail. Black Theology must seriously consider the cultural expressions of the people it represents so that it will be able to speak relevantly to the black condition. Jon Spencer has identified what black theologians have labeled "theomusicology."

> A musicological method for theologizing about the sacred (the religious/churched), the secular (the theistic, unreligious/unchurched), and the profane (the atheistic/irreligious)—including sacred and non-sacred music functioning as theomusico-therapy in church and community—principally incorporating methods borrowed from anthropology, sociology, psychology, and philosophy.[16]

With Black Theology being the theme of this study, and the emphasis placed on liberation, Garth Baker-Fletcher states, "A kind of revolution is happening, described by rappers with a back-burner beat of hip-hop rhythm, moving the minds, bodies, and feet of the

---

14. Cone, *The Cross and the Lynching Tree*, 118.
15. West, *Prophetic Thought in Postmodern Times*, 69.
16. Spencer, Preface to *The Theology of American Popular Music*, vii.

masses away from the control of the system toward a new place."[17] This revolution did not have its beginnings in today's culture, but begin prophetically with slavery and now is at a spatial time in history where fulfillment is imminent. "This is not to argue that the contrasting moral frameworks of rap and religion do not color our interpretation of their often-opposing creeds. But we must not forget that unpopular and unacceptable views are sometimes later regarded as prophetic."[18] Hodge agrees by stating this about hip-hop icon, Tupac: "Tupac was a street prophet, one who could connect the hood and the thug to God through life, language, music and community. Tupac offered the hood a higher glimpse of the future. He functioned as a post-soul saint for those who view God from the gutter."[19]

"Swing Low Sweet Chariot" is one of the most classic of "negro slave" spiritual songs. The song voiced hope of freedom in a heavenly home after death. The most notable rap song for this hip-hop generation that expresses the same hope is Bone Thugs-N-Harmony's "Tha Crossroads," the timeless correlation of how death is not a consequence of oppression, but is an *antecedent* to the freedom of that oppression. Language is an arbitrary system of assigning meaning to life, culture, and context; the language used in these two songs relates how two different cultures view the same thing (death) using different languages in their contexts. According to Daniel White Hodge, this song by Bone Thugs-N-Harmony encouraged their listeners to have a relationship with God and follow the instructions to work their "plan" for entrance into heaven and see death as only a doorway into another dimension. The next generations of hip-hoppers are seeing the society, the church, and themselves through a different lens and they seek spirituality that speaks directly to them. Their voice is not speaking through the theology of orthodox Christianity because they believe traditional Christianity has betrayed them with complacency and silence. Black Theology, like Holy Hip-hop, is not a black thing, but, in

17. Fletcher, *Xodus*, 175.

18. Dyson, *Holler If You Hear Me*, 209.

19. Hodge, *The Soul of Hip-hop*, 142.

fact, is a God thing, and when the oppression of black people becomes a matter of the past, the oppression of all oppressed people passes. When injustice for black people is not the color of their skin, the injustice for all people will be de-colored.

A new rhetoric of Black Theology finds the hungry ears of the youth of the inner-city, both black and brown. The true nature of the street must be matched with the culture of the community. The ghettos and barrios of the city live by a different set of rules. No one church can change the landscape of injustice, oppression, and poverty. No one church can heal the wounds of the American sin of slavery; no one church can expect to bring salvation and deliverance to those with no hope; it will take the church; one body, one bride of Christ, one blood and one cross.

The church should be ashamed and appalled the old Jim Crow system of oppression, injustice, and racism has resurrected itself in a penal system disguised in the raiment of American Justice. The outward cry of the Civil Rights Movement, "Free at Last, Free at Last," becomes muted by the shouts of the New Jim Crow, "Law and Order, Law and Order." But there is another voice shouting across the yawning gaping abyss of the search for freedom and equality, and that voice is the next generation of worshippers who are shouting with a loud voice, "No Justice, No Peace, No Justice, No Peace," and this voice must speak in the rhetoric of Black Theology. Life, liberty, and the pursuit of happiness becomes a lie in the face of constitutional truths. All people are created equally, but not all people stay equal. The egalitarianism of the will of the people becomes unbalanced on the scales of justice.

Different theologies teach different understandings about God, but that understanding has to be contextualized to the listening ear of the hearer. As particular attention focuses on the inner-city, traditional Christianity that professes turning the other cheek is not effective or useful for spiritual formation. Mixing faith conversation with the militancy of Malcolm X and the hope of Martin L. King, Jr. will bring hope and identity with Christ and will show them a God who cares for His poor, oppressed, and disenfranchised people. This identification cannot be done easily outside the rhetoric of Black Theology in the inner-city. Since hip-hop is an international language of youth, the combination of Black Theology and Holy Hip-hop will assist youth to learn how to love God with all their heart, all their souls, all their mind, and all their strength (Mark 12: 30).

# ETHNOMETHODOLOGY—
## THE ABNORMALITY OF NORMALCY

# CHAPTER 6

# Relevant Social Analysis

A NUMBER OF SOCIAL facts have been documented and made available for researchers who are interested in sociological interpretations of the inner-city. Fortunately, the documentation of these facts are accessible at the common sense level so that the nonspecialist can draw out implications and conclusions in support of related studies. It was necessary to draw upon these studies to describe factors that impact the inner-city and shape its relationship to the rest of society. The data examined in this chapter will assist a better understanding of social conditions that are largely unacknowledged and unaddressed in the mainline church.

Three questions will be raised in this chapter:

1. Is it the responsibility of the church to get involved with these "worldly/secular" issues?

2. How does the church affect change in these situations?

3. What help does Black Theology and Holy Hip-hop offer in shaping the church's response to these situations?

It is important to realize that, at least in perception, nothing is being done to correct these issues and no known governmental effective agenda is established to resolve the current problems. The escalating level of these social pathologies has created an ever-widening gap between the haves and have-nots in American society. Growing mistrust and anguish influences the minds and actions of people who feel oppressed and left out of the "American Dream."

The data presented here is not new. The level of failure in the obligation to meet social need and the measurements that show it are well known; there are so surprises. Martin Luther King Jr. complains:

> The church has often lagged in its concern for social justice and too often has been content to mouth pious irrelevancies and sanctimonious trivialities. It has often been so absorbed in a future good "over yonder" that it forgets the present evils "down here." Yet the church is challenged to make the gospel of Jesus Christ relevant with the social situation. We must come to see that the Christian gospel is a two-way road. On one side, it seeks to change the souls of men and thereby unite them with God; on the other, it seeks to change the environmental conditions of men so that the soul will have a chance after it is changed.[1]

Cone argues the church and Christians have not adequately demonstrated that their theory (theology) and practice (discipleship/doing of the Word) are always consistent. Many within the ecclesiastical community are aware of the data presented here, but the church still pays inadequate attention to the "least of these" (Matt 25:45). Cone argues:

> The only real question for Christians is whether their actions are in harmony with their knowledge of God. And the only ones who are in a position to answer the question concerning the epistemological justification of the knowledge of God are the members of a given Christian community. Others with some empathy may give an intellectual evaluation of the perspective of the community, but they cannot tell the community what is or is not true and expect the community to take it seriously.[2]

Among the first issues to be examined are sub-standard educational opportunities and their effect on inner-city ministry. Several studies have pointed out that educational inequities have

---

1. King, *Strength to Love*, 104.
2. Cone, A *Black Theology of Liberation*, 41.

led to gross economic gaps and contributed to poverty and social inequities among black and brown people. As a result, what is real outside the school does not affect what is taught inside the school, thereby making education unrealistic. The truth about life is lost in the boredom of non-stimulating intellectual discussions, making education irrelevant. Therefore, school has no value for black and brown youth, and where there is no value, there is no participation, thus making education worthless and unnecessary.

The No Child Left Behind Act (NCLB) of 2002 was a federal law proposed by President George Bush, which legislated funds aimed at improving the performance of U.S. schools by increasing standards of accountability as well as providing parents flexibility in choosing which schools their children will attend. The overall intent of the NCLB is that all children achieve a state standard to reach their full potential. In order to meet these goals, the NCLB has divided its funding into "titles" aimed at equal opportunity for all students regardless of race, gender, and as Secretary Margaret Spellings indicated, zip codes. In brief, these titles include the following:

1. Title I, Part A supports programs and resources for disadvantaged students. Title 1A funding is designed to aid districts in closing the achievement gap by placing highly qualified teachers in classrooms.

2. Title I, Part D is designed to serve delinquent and neglected youth in institutions, day programs, and correctional facilities to assure they attain high academic levels of achievement.

3. Title II, Part A provides resources for improving teacher and principal quality. It focuses on preparing, training, and recruiting high-quality teachers and principals.

4. Title II, Part D facilitates improved student academic achievement through the use of technology in schools.

5. Title IV, Part A provides resources for fostering a safe and drug-free learning environment that supports academic achievement.[3]

The overall failure of NCLB has not gone undocumented within the last 10 years of its existence, and additionally, it should be noted that the unequal social/education gaps which prompted the NCLB existed in 1965 Watts Riots, thirty-six years prior to NCLB, 1992 Compton Riots, nine years prior, and are still present in 2015, fourteen years after NCLB was implemented, especially in particular zip codes. Lisa Guisbond, a policy analyst, and Monty Neill, an executive director, along with Bob Schaeffer, a public education director, all from the National Center for Fair and Open Testing in Boston, whose aim it is to end the misuse of standardized testing, have written an assessment of the NCLB. In their article, "NCLB's Lost Decade for Educational Progress: What Can We Learn from this Policy Failure," commented,

> A review of a decade of evidence demonstrates that NCLB has failed badly both in terms of its own goals and more broadly. It has neither significantly increased academic performance nor significantly reduced achievement gaps, even as measured by standardized exams. It is time to acknowledge this failure and adopt a more effective course for the federal role in education and pursue proven alternatives to guide and support the nation's neediest schools and students. NCLB has 1) severely damaged educational quality and equity, with its narrowing and limiting effects failing most severely on the poor. 2) Failed to significantly increase average academic performance and significantly narrow achievement gaps. 3) Failed to address many of its fundamental flaws and in some cases will intensify them. These proposals will extend a "lost decade for U.S. schools."[4]

3. Orange County Vocational Technical School, "No Child Left Behind Act Summary," [Report, January 8, 2002] (New Jersey: Department of Education, 2002), available from http://www.ocvts.org/webdocs/district . . . /nochildleft-behind-summary-pdf.pdf Internet, accessed 14, September, 2014.

4. Guisbond, "NCLB's Lost Decade for Educational Progress."

The examination of this apparent failure of NCLB and its effect on the inner-city makes it clear that money and racism are still overshadowing the success of inner-city black and brown youth. Is one of the largest problems associated with this fallacy of NCLB one of fix or measure? Is it truly possible for the youth in inner-city neighborhoods to come up to the "standardized" levels outlined in the NCLB mandate in the year of 2015? Deborah Meier et al. have argued that despite the good intentions of improving public schools and increasing the ability of the system to serve the poor and minority children, NCLB is doing the opposite. "The wealthiest U.S. public schools spend at least ten times more than the poorest schools-ranging from over $30,000 per pupil at the wealthy schools to only $3,000 at the poorest. These disparities contribute to a wider achievement gap in this country."[5]

Studies have demonstrated that the wealthier school districts which tend to have lower percentages of black and brown low income students tend to have the highest graduation rate of each of those students respectively; in other words, the lower percentage of black and brown students, the more the percentage of proficiency. Education Trust-West is an organization in Oakland, California which measures and monitors opportunity and achievement gaps that separate students of color and low-income students from other youth, and advocate strategies that will close those gaps.

> Only 1 percent of students in San Marino Unified is African-American, 3 percent of students are low-income, and 94 percent of African American students are proficient in English language arts. Meanwhile, a quarter of students in Eastside Union Elementary is African-American, and the majority of students are low-income. But only a third of African-American students are proficient.[6]

Furthermore, with regard to the irony of "standardized" testing utilized by NCLB, he argues that "Standardized tests are used to determine everything from whether students will be allowed to receive a diploma to whether schools themselves will be allowed

5. Meier et.al., *Many Children Left Behind*, 6.
6. Education Trust-West, *At A Crossroad*, 4.

to continue operating to where students will be able to go to college (if at all).[7] Therefore, it appears that NCLB is another political instrument to measure the successfulness of inner-city schools compared to other schools that have better resources, teachers, finances and technology by holding them to a standard they cannot reach, thereby labeling students and schools as "failing."

According to Title 1, Part A and Title II, Part A, NCLB promises to provide appropriate and skilled teachers to "disadvantaged" low-income schools, however; there has been a significant failure in that area also. Linda Darling Hammon concludes in her research that African-American students in high-poverty, high-minority schools receive less of everything that matters most in education including effective resources and teachers.[8] Entwisle, Alexander, and Olson argue that students in intensely segregated schools are almost three times as likely to have a teacher lacking full qualifications than students attending majority white and Asian schools.[9] Teacher quality and motivation are important to the learning process and student morale. A "hands off" or "passing through" attitude of those in authority and teaching positions are perceived by students as it undermines an ability to learn. Additionally, research completed by the Department of Education reveals the lack of teacher preparedness and skill level in the inner-city to be a part of the failure of NCLB.

Sixty years after Brown v. Board of Education, black and brown youth still suffer in a separate but unequal education system. What makes inner-city schools segregated today? Education Trust-West states,

> African-Americans often attend schools where they are substantially overrepresented and that are intensely segregated (defined as schools where more than 90 percent of students come from underrepresented minority backgrounds). African-American students are also more likely to enroll in largely Latino neighborhood schools,

7. Wise, *Dear White America*, 34.

8. Hammond, "Inequality and the Right to Learn."

9. Entwisle, et al., *Children, Schools, and Inequality*, 208.

where they are a declining minority in schools that face both racial and socioeconomic isolation.[10]

Education Trust-West reports that the demographic make-up of Los Angeles County at one point indicated that African-American students used to be the third largest subgroup in Los Angeles County, making up about twelve percent of the student population in 1994. Currently, nine percent of students are African-Americans and nearly three-quarters of these students are socioeconomically disadvantaged. Many districts that used to serve large percentages of African-American students, such as Compton Unified, have seen dramatic decreases in African-American enrollment (from 33 percent to 17 percent) and large increases in Latino enrollment (from 46 percent to 79 percent of the student population) since 2000.[11]

White America has long argued that money isn't really what makes a difference in schools—and therefore, inequities in resources aren't really the problem—we must also acknowledge that none of us are clamoring to switch places or to have our kids switch places with the students of color who attend less well-funded institutions, hoping to make up for the difference with good values and a solid work ethic. As is often the case, those who say money doesn't matter typically have money, so to them, it doesn't matter.[12]

Title IV, Part A of NCLB provides resources for fostering a safe and drug-free learning environment that supports academic achievement, which is another miserable failure. A lawsuit that involved Luther Burbank Middle School, which serves low-income students of color in San Francisco, opened an EEO case. The plaintiffs in Williams v. California identified conditions that are not uncommon to inner-city schools in Los Angeles. Many students in the inner-city cannot take textbooks home because there is only enough for class time only; homework is photocopied as handouts and does not contain guides or references. Some history and

---

10. Education Trust-West, *At A Crossroads*, 8.

11. Ibid., 2.

12. Wise, *Dear White America*, 34.

political science text books are outdated and do not contain the most relevant information to support the type of testing required by NCLB conditions not to be labeled as "failing." Water and bathroom facilities are inadequate and unsanitary while the landscape of the school resembles more of a prison than a place of learning. Violence on school campuses is prevalent and common-place.

The violence in Los Angeles County Unified School District is directly related to the drop-out rates and those rates are related to the suspension rates of that district. Although a fundamental understanding of suspension is to correct student behavior and thereby lower the likelihood of more serious involvement in the juvenile justice system, that result is unlikely. Many black and brown youth in the inner-city see the suspension process of schools as a precursor to the ultimate court system outside the school. Commit a crime (school fighting or vandalism) then stand before the principal (judge) defending against a prosecutor (counselor or vice principal) against an accuser (victim) with an outcome of discipline or punishment (suspension) or expulsion from school (jail). Education Trust-West suggests,

> In Los Angeles Unified, for example, African-American male suspension rates were 18 percentage points higher than white male suspension rates (23 percent versus 5 percent). The California Department of Justice reports in L.A. County a much larger share of African-American students is arrested for felony charges than white students. Specifically, for every 1,000 youth ages 10-17, 38 African-American juveniles are arrested for felonies, as compared with 7 white youth.[13]

The long term effect of this parallel system in schools has long range damage to the life of the black and brown students who are routinely denied public benefits and the freedom to education instead of prison, inequality instead of American egalitarianism, and self-worth instead of poverty.

When you live in poverty, you fight as though everything has or will be taken away from you. There is an emotional conviction

13. Education Trust-West, *At A Crossroads,* 7.

of guilt and anger; guilt because you are here and angry because you seem powerless to make a change. For some students, violence is a part of life. Parents are abusive, friends are abusive; violent behavior is a learned and accepted part of normal life. Inner-city culture says it is acceptable to be violent while at the same time saying it is dangerous not to be violent. Book bags contain books, pencils, notebooks, and in some cases a weapon. In California, the first state to require school districts to keep statistics on school crime, the Department of Education (1989) reported that assaults in schools increased by sixteen percent in the four years ending with the 1988-89 school year; incidents of weapons possession rose by twenty-eight percent.

The abysmal failure of the NCLB program with regard to education in the inner-city leads directly to poor employment opportunities. The following table indicates that black men, even more than Hispanic men, remain concentrated in the lower rungs of the test core distribution. This correlation and the concentration of young blacks and Hispanics near the bottom of the test score distribution suggest that a considerable "mismatch" remains between the skills sought by employers—especially for jobs that pay well—and those held by young black and Hispanic men.

## Test Scores and Employment Rates for Young Men, Ages 16 to 24, 1994

|  | White | Black | Hispanic |
|---|---|---|---|
| *Test scores (%)* |  |  |  |
| Below the 20th percentile | 24.5 | 54.1 | 41.2 |
| 20th to 49th percentile | 37.4 | 30.5 | 42.2 |
| 50th to 79th percentile | 27.9 | 13.3 | 13.0 |
| 80th percentile and above | 10.3 | 2.1 | 3.6 |

|  | White | Black | Hispanic |
|---|---|---|---|
| *Employment* | | | |
| Below the 20th percentile | 74.0 | 47.7 | 57.4 |
| 20th to 49th percentile | 78.0 | 67.2 | 69.0 |
| 50th to 79th percentile | 79.7 | 61.4 | 77.6 |
| 80th percentile and above | 73.6 | 87.3 | 84.0 |
| *Employment, high school graduates* | | | |
| Below 50th percentile and above | 83.3 | 71.3 | 72.5 |
| 50th percentile and above | 80.8 | 74.2 | 79.6 |
| *Employment, high school dropouts* | | | |
| Below 50th percentile | 66.3 | 37.9 | 53.9 |
| 50th percentile and above | 69.0 | 33.9 | 76.8 |

*Note:* Test scores are from a basic cognitive skills test administered as part of the NELS. The sample excludes students enrolled in postsecondary education, those without 1988 test score data, and those without employment data. Since those enrolled in college are excluded from this sample, the distribution of test scores is skewed toward the bottom (i.e. more than 20 percent of the sample will fall below the 20th percentile, etc.) Source: The National Center for Education Statistics, National Educational Longitudinal Survey (1994).

Peter Edelman, Harry J. Holzer and Paul Offner argue:

The data lead us to a twofold conclusion. First, educational attainment and cognitive skills contribute heavily to earnings and employment gaps between young whites and minorities, and must figure prominently in any discussion of policy responses. Second, gaps in early work experience between young black men and others, which appear unrelated to education and basic skills, also develop early and persist over time. Research as focused on the "spatial mismatch" between jobs that are increasingly located in distant suburbs and the continued concentration of black residences in segregated inner-city neighborhoods. Apparently, young inner-city blacks not only lack easy transportation to areas of high suburban job growth, but also information about such jobs.[14]

Edelman, Holzer, and Offner point out that employer's fear conflict with young black men, and they complain about poor attitudes toward work and authority. No doubt some of these employers' attitudes reflect traditional negative stereotypes and racism. Alienation from mainstream values and institutions seems strong, especially as articulated in the street (or 'hip-hop') culture of the young. By at least some accounts, the peer culture of disadvantaged minority youth treats school achievement as "acting white."

But what does all this have to do with the church? Can the church truly set free those locked in educational jail cells looking through bars of oppression into a world that does not see them other than criminals or uneducated an unequal "them." Peter J. Paris states:

> The black churches long believed that the education of blacks was not a mere end in itself, but instead a means for changing white public opinion about blacks. All believed that if whites would see more and more blacks embodying gentle manners, excellence in speech, good moral character, industry, and good-will, they would cease stereotyping blacks according to the boisterous behavior of the black masses.[15]

A philosophy of education should focus on the primary goal of holistic repair and intellectually challenging the environment of the current educational system found in the inner-city context. If what the church can do today through education is provide new hope and a renewed energy for learning, then it has a chance to move the people of the inner-city from secularity and obscurity to the promise land of truth, reality, and value found in the Word of God.

There are certain challenges related to adult learning. These challenges become more apparent in the inner-city environment. The conditions of survival have taken priority over the privileges

---

14. Edelman et al., *Reconnecting Disadvantaged Young Men*, 22.

15. Paris, *The Social Teaching of the Black Churches*, 68.

of education. The hope of success in the educational system is lost in those conditions of survival. When inner-city youth and adults are not in school, they face the harsh realities of the failure in their community due to violence, drugs, poverty, unemployment, and dysfunctional families. Kitty Kelly Epstein states:

> Many Americans have abandoned even the hope of fairness in the marketplace, the bureaucracy, and the health care system. But they still expect schools to be fair, to provide opportunity, justice, skills and enlightenment. And when the schools are not fair and nurturing, people are willing to struggle about the ideas and issues which under gird this failure.[16]

These studies are important to the current research because they illustrate the lack and failure of public policy to educate inner-city people, therefore making them unreceptive to Christian belief. Additionally, these studies point to a socio/theological challenge to the church. The church must challenge the political structures that oppress the life, liberty, and pursuit of happiness guaranteed by the constitution. Peter J. Paris makes the following statement, "Black churches have believed that the task of racial uplift (educationally and morally) lay basically in the hands of blacks themselves, and consequently their schools became the prime exemplars of that viewpoint."[17]

Graduate theological students, whose primary aim is evangelization in the inner-city, will not be received. Furthermore, it is not evangelization that is needed in the inner-city, it is educational and economic opportunity; if this could be provided through faith in the church, there is greater identification with God in this effort. It requires a firm movement from the class room to the streets; as Kauffman and Elliston state, ". . . they must learn what loving your neighbor means in a crowded tenement, a sprawling third-world slum, and in neighborhoods where crime and poverty are as thick as flies on the garbage."[18]

16. Epstein, *A Different View of Urban Schools,* 84.

17. Paris, *The Social Teaching of the Black Churches,* 69.

18. Elliston and Kauffman, *Developing Leaders for Urban Ministries,* 144.

Arlene Sanchez Walsh makes clear how the church should address the challenge for intellectual development among community congregants. She states,

> Perhaps if we in the academy take up the task of becoming evangelists of a different kind, insisting on the broadening of our minds, the feeding of our intellectual curiosity, and the opening of our faith to interlopers, we will go a long way to completing the triad of commands the LORD has asked of us: Love the LORD with all your heart, all your soul, and all your mind. To me, it is a command worthy of our efforts.[19]

---

19. Sanchez-Walsh. *Latino Pentecostal Identity,* 194.

# CHAPTER 7

# The Crucifixion of the Evangelical Inner-City Mind

IT WAS MALCOLM X who coined the phrase, "A Mind is a terrible thing to waste," and this phrase was used as part of a campaign slogan by the United Negro College Fund in 1972. The words are designed to encourage people to seek higher education, and place a deep sense of responsibility on a person to perform to the highest level of their potential. But the mind can be a product of its environment and in an effort to protect itself from harmful pathology will develop "coping" mechanisms of survival. Lerone Bennett, executive editor of Ebony Magazine says, "The question of education for Black people in America is a question of life and death. It is a political question, a question of power. Struggle is a form of education, perhaps the highest form."[1]

Within the inner-city context, where the bulk of black and brown people are concentrated, there is currently a "Jim Crow" separate but equal system that is obviously theorized as a design to perpetuate a sense of class inferiority through an image reminiscent of slavery. Is it conceivable that slavery still has an adverse effect on the thinking of inner-city people? How much does a slavery mindset influence a theological thinking of Jesus Christ or has an inner-city evangelical mind been crucified but not resurrected through the work of the cross? Harvard educated and trained W.E.B. DuBois made the following observation:

---

1. Bennett, *The Challenge of Blackness*, 228.

> A separate Negro school where children are treated like
> human beings, trained by teachers of their own race, who
> know what it means to be black in the year of salvation
> 1935, is infinitely better than making our boys and girls
> doormats to be spit and trampled upon and lied to by
> ignorant social climbers, whose sole claim to superiority
> is ability to kick "niggers" when they are down.[2]

Although this seems to be a very strong statement supporting
Jim Crow separatist policy of slavery, Dubois' statement is not an
indictment for separate schools, but rather a cry for the need of
quality education for all. Since 1935, there has been a significant
growth toward this goal and many black and brown students have
been admitted and graduated from some of the most prestigious
black colleges in the nation. The focus here is not on those who
have "made it" but more importantly on those who have been
"forgotten" and have formed a negative criticism of God through
non-involvement or participation in the relational aspects of evangelical thinking.

George Woodson argues to provide black youth (and brown
youth indirectly) access to historical information and education
which would nullify or at least diminish belittling ideas of inferiority would help them better rationalize a history which has been
handed down to them by whites, particularly through the program
of the Willie Lynch letter. His work was written during the time
of President Woodrow Wilson when separate but equal afforded
respectable legal sanctions for an unequal, caste-like society, in
education where a silent participation resigned itself over much
of the black population.[3] Unfortunately, this unspoken acceptance
was also present in the church, and many believed that the character of education at that time (and presently) was at least "better
than it used to be." Gutierrez makes the following statement:

> There are still black preachers who argue that they do not
> need any training in theology in order to preach the gos-
> pel. That may have been an acceptable position in days

2. Dubois, "Does the Negro Need Separate Schools?" 335.

3. Woodson, *The Mis-Education of the Negro*, 9.

past when there was little or no opportunity for formal study. But not today. Black preachers who think so have confused the gospel of Jesus with their own distorted piety or personal interest. Some black preachers do not know how to distinguish between black faith and white religion; without a critical black theology that can distinguish good religion from bad religion, black preachers are left with the option of simply imitating the false gods of the electronic church in order to keep their congregations from deserting the 11: 00 am service and other activities of their churches.[4]

This thought of "all I need is the Holy Ghost to be my teacher," is connected with the perception that seminaries are really "cemeteries" where faith is castrated in the name of academia. The "Black Church" has long separated itself from formal and theological education on the pretense of it being a "white man's education and religion" and these schisms add to the classicism evident in the inner-city context. Carter Woodson commented:

> In schools of theology Negroes are taught the interpretation of the Bible worked out by those who have justified segregation and winked at the economic debasement of the Negro sometimes almost to the point of starvation. Deriving their sense of right from this teaching, graduates of such schools can have no message to grip the people whom they have been ill-trained to serve. Most of such mis-educated ministers, therefore, preach to benches while illiterate Negro preachers do the best they can in supplying the spiritual needs of the masses.[5]

The paradox of the spirituality of the Black church and the academic representation of Black Theology in schools becomes an enigma to the inner-city evangelical mindset. It can be compared to the example of how Thomas Jefferson could be both a slaveholder and a champion of liberty. Cone argues:

---

4. Gutierrez, *The Power of the Poor in History*, 45.
5. Woodson, *The Mis-Education of the Negro*, 17–18.

> There is some disagreement between the black church
> and its relationship to black theology. That is, to some
> degree, a paradox of words "black theology" and "black
> church;" the two should not be in an antagonistic rela-
> tionship by the very nature of the words "theology" and
> "church" with the transitive adjective "black." Is black
> theology, therefore, an academic discipline or a prophetic
> understanding of the activity of God in black thought?[6]

Theologically Cone's argument is about relationship; that
is, the academic necessity of Black Theology and the prophetic
revelation of God's activity through the Black church balance
the commandment of Jesus (Matt 22:37). But educationally, how
does the relationship of teacher/student dyad affect the learning
outcome in the critical evaluation of pedagogy? How much of the
internal values of the teacher manifest themselves in the external
psychological dynamic of the student? Joseph L. White, a noted
psychologist, identified primary dimensions in the psychological space of Afro-Americans. White argues that openness to self
and others, tragedy and resilience, psychological connectedness
and interdependence, the oral tradition, creative synthesis, fluid
time perception, the value of direct experience, and respect for the
elderly are all dimensions that constitute a definitive black ethos.

As White continues to speak of this educational relationship
he argues, "When it comes to the match between white teachers
and black students, a number of historical and socio-cultural factors at work in the backgrounds of white teachers prevent them
from being able to create a psychological climate characterized by
the facilitative conditions of genuineness, positive regard, and empathic understanding in their relationships with black students."[7]
White makes it clear that there are three factors that contribute
to this dynamic relationship. First, there is the racism inherent in
American society.

In other words, the attitudes of black inferiority on the part of
white teachers, whether explicit or implicit, prevent teachers from

6. Cone, *For My People*, 99.

7. White, *The Psychology of Blacks*, 117.

seeing the intellectual strengths in black students (a point argued in the previous discussion of Willie Lynch letter.) As discussed by Emerson and Smith, the difference between individual racism and a racialized society or structure makes an impact on how this inferiority is conceptualized. "Many humanitarian liberal white teachers, those who love and want to save all poor black folks, attempt to shield black students from failure by shielding black student's failure by imposing a permanent set of lowered expectations is only another way of communicating to them that they are not capable of achieving."[8]

Secondly, according to White, black students may not closely approximate the Anglo teacher's ideal of what a good student acts like, talks like, and walks like. This is translated in the perceptions of stereotypes. These cultural differences in the behavioral styles of white teachers and inner-city youth are a potential source of conflict. The final divisive factor, according to White, in the relationship between black students and white teachers is in the students' cultural background, which values human relationships, feelings, genuineness, and emotional closeness. To reconcile this relationship schism, love seems to be the foundation for teaching effectively. "You cannot teach a child you do not love. You cannot teach a child you do not respect. You cannot teach a child you do not understand. You cannot teach a child you fear. You cannot teach a child before discarding your political baggage. You cannot teach a child without bonding with him first. To bond, you must have love, respect and understanding. When you teach Black boys, what do you see? Whatever you see will be what you produce."[9]

The implications of these arguments serve to highlight that racism is at the heart of educational discrepancies of black and brown youth in the inner-city context. Furthermore, those educational discrepancies tend to crucify a theological understanding of faith. Education is directly related to black thought; black thought is directly tied to black identity and self-worth; black identity and self-worth is directly related to a clear articulated knowledge of

8. Ibid., 118.

9. Kunjufu, *Countering the Conspiracy to Destroy Black Boys*, 22.

God. Before an understanding can be gained in relation to the church and God, clarity must be established as to how much racism vis-a-vis education is related to economics and black culture. When education is sacrificed in the name of the status quo, it also extends to economic oppression of inner-city life and family. The dichotomies of salvation and survival, war and battles, and African-Americans and street *niggas*, is directly proportional to the amount of income one earns. In order to close the classicism of the inner-city, the gaps must be closed on racist practices that divide and conquer the people of the inner-city. In order to defuse the anger of black and brown youth in the inner-city, there must be a way to increase self-esteem, build relationships and repair families by providing ways for family needs and provisions, without the use of violence and drugs.

Traditional Christianity does not speak to the current issues as mentioned above or in an effort to do so have not spoken with a rhetoric that makes the residents of the inner-city confident that a change is coming to save them from the captivity of oppression, poverty, injustice, employment inequality, and environmental devastation. This has to be a goal of Black Theology as there have been no other voices of theological reference that have had or spoken the rhetoric of liberation. Emerson and Smith argue:

> Because evangelicals view their primary task as evangelism and discipleship, they tend to avoid issues that hinder these activities. Thus, they are generally not counter-cultural. They avoid "rocking the boat," and live within the confines of the larger culture. At times they have been able to call for and realize social change, but most typically their influence has been limited to alterations at the margins. So, despite having sub cultural tools to call for radical changes in race relations, they most consistently call for changes in persons that leave the dominant social structures, institutions, and culture intact.[10]

10. Emerson and Smith, *Divided by Faith*, 21.

What is the origin of this schism of involvement in the black dilemma? Where did America go wrong and how does America fix the problem? Cone presents one side of the dichotomy while Emerson and Smith present another side; yet the inner-city evangelical mind is confused and often combative during this ecclesiastical schizophrenic theological episode. Many scholars wonder why black people cannot get past the slavery issue that happened so long ago. Some doubt that this American sin can still have damaging effects upon the psychological pathology of black people in this perceived "colorblind" society. Tim Wise has stated:

> Naturally, none of us [white America] who worry about people of color adopting a debilitating mindset of victimhood ever fret about the same thing happening to others who have been victimized by injustice. We don't tell Jewish folks to get over the Holocaust, or not to talk about those unhappy matters, lest they cripple themselves under the weight of a victim syndrome. Keep in mind that there has been steady support for curricula that address the destruction of European Jewry under Hitler, and no one as suggested teaching the Diary of Anne Frank might be debilitating to Jewish children. So why is it acceptable for these other groups' members to focus on their victimization, while it's somehow untoward or even self-destructive for people of color to do so?[11]

Something has happened to silence the voice and quail the rhetoric of reconciliation theology. A deliberate acquiescence over the years have regressed the evangelical energy of race conscientiousness in America. This is clearly demonstrated in the following two statements of Billy Graham and Cecil "Chip" Murray. Billy Graham shares in the blame and writes that evangelical Christians "too often in the past. . .turned a blind eye to racism."

> Because racism is a sin, it is a moral and spiritual issue. . .only the supernatural love of God can change our hearts in a lasting way and replace hatred and indifference with love and active compassion. No other

11. Wise, *Dear White America*, 59.

force exists besides the church that can bring people together. . .Of all people, Christians should be the most active in reaching out to those of other races, instead of accepting the status quo of division and animosity.[12]

What happened to the reconciliation message? What turned the hearts of this message that spread to a white audience? In 1997, the Promise Keepers held a large stadium event in Washington D.C., called "Stand in the Gap: A Sacred Assembly." It was reported that between 500,000 and one million men attended this event and it emphasized reconciliation as one of its core themes.[13] After all this activity and moving forward toward reconciliation, frustration was apparent in the following statement by Cecil "Chip" Murray, "White evangelicals need an at-risk gospel. . .Calling sinners to repentance means also calling societies and structures to repentance-economic, social, educational, corporate, political, religious structures. . .The gospel at once works with individual and the individual's society: to change one, we of necessity must change the other."[14]

The break-down of racial reconciliation among evangelicals is epitomized in the theology of "individual sin." This theology embraces the concept that each person is individually responsible for their own involvement or non-involvement in the racial problem in America and this theology comes from the "original sin" of the fall with Adam and Eve. That is, the major component of reconciliation of the founding fathers challenging social systems of injustice and inequality, confession of social sin, is almost absent in light of this theology of individualism. "Most evangelicals, even in the North (during the Jim Crow era) did not think it their duty to oppose segregation; it was enough to treat blacks they knew personally with courtesy and fairness."[15] Therefore, the racism which is not individual (that is racialized society) is not challenged; what is challenged is the treatment of individuals within the system;

12. Graham, "Racism and the Evangelical Church," 27.

13. Emerson and Smith, *Divided by Faith,* 66.

14. Murray, "Needed: An At-Risk Gospel," 20.

15. Martin, *A Prophet with Honor,* 168.

therefore, if the system is broken, it is broken because of broken individuals. As seen from the position of Emerson and Smith, evangelicals see the race problem from three perspectives:

> For them, the race problem is one or more of three main types: (1) prejudiced individuals, resulting in bad relationships and sin, (2) other groups-usually African Americans-trying to make race problems a group issue when there is nothing more than individual problems, and (3) a fabrication of the self-interested—again often African-Americans, but also the media, the government, or liberals.[16]

Racism is therefore not systemic, but endemic. This flow of logic does not make sense in light of the fact that systems of oppression are not ecclesiastically "owned;" therefore to change the mind of a single individual does not in effect change the practice of the system and to collectively change the practice of the system means to change the mind collectively of those who "own" the system (typically non-believers) and collectively this change (repentance) can only happen socially and politically.

It is interesting to see that each of the points addressed by Emerson and Smith on the race problem in America from an evangelical position and the views of the race problem as addressed by Tim Wise from the typical white American point of view have focused on systems that black people do not "own" nor have any control over. If there is no resolve from the theological (evangelical) point of view of racism and that same similar thought is on the hearts of non-evangelical (white America), then where does the inner-city evangelical mind find resolution? Evangelicals in the inner-city do not see race as white evangelicals do and surely do not see the race problem as typical white America does. Does resolve come from sin or salvation?

It can be confirmed that traditional evangelical thought with regard to the race problem is also due largely to isolation. The racial homogenous world of evangelicalism (outside of what is seen in mainstream media) shelters them and does not expose them

16. Emerson and Smith, *Divided by Faith*, 74.

to racial diversity; furthermore, they are insulated in their own world and consequently, they do not witness street-level racism and prejudice. Therefore, the race problem cannot be as large or severe as those locked in the confines of its cells are making it out to be. Individualism and isolation are at the root of evangelical complacency and apathy to the race problem in America and so also in the church. Emerson and Smith make this claim:

> The cultural tools and intergroup isolation of evangelicals lead them to construct reality so as to individualize and minimize the problem. It is a necessity for evangelicals to interpret the problem at the individual level. To do so otherwise would challenge the very basis of their world, both their faith and the American way of life. Suggesting social causes of the race problem challenges the cultural elements with which they construct their lives. Because reality is socially constructed, a highly effective way to ensure the perpetuation of a racialized system is simply to deny its existence. Contemporaries are not doing this out of some old form of Jim Crow racism with no apparent intent; the result is the maintenance of a racialized United States.[17]

If evangelicals see a race problem, but do not hear the cries of God's people under the oppressive hands of injustice and inequality and do not answer the call of God to deliver His people, then evangelicals suffer from a "silence of the lambs" fallacy. This fallacy acknowledges the problem of racism, but chooses not to speak against it. It is a fallacy that sees silence as the defense for this offensive behavior against the community of God. It is a fallacy of look but do not touch; ignore but do not confront. It is a fallacy where the voice of God is muted in the uproarious sounds of American patriotism—it is a silence of the lamb's fallacy that undermines intelligence and worships the complacency of apathetic theological double-mindedness.

The silence of the lamb's fallacy not only mutes the voices that cry for freedom, but blinds the eyes to the reality of oppression.

17. Emerson and Smith, *Divided by Faith*, 89–90.

The fallacy misses the fact that some races can live anywhere they want, walk down any street and not be concerned with the fact they are not wanted. The fallacy misses the fact that most, black and brown men, cannot walk down the street without a "stop and frisk" suspicion of criminality. The fallacy misses that [white America] are far more likely than black and brown Americans to get a quality education. The fallacy misses the fact that white Americans are twice more likely to get fair treatment by the court systems than black and brown Americans. The fallacy announces that if it cannot be heard, it cannot be seen. Tim Wise puts it this way:

> In effect, we [white America] have placed noise-canceling headphones over our ears, letting in only the pleasant sounds we wish to hear, while shutting out the rest. So the dulcet tones of patriotism, the self-congratulatory rhythms of American exceptionalism have soothed us to the point of inducing a collective coma, a hypnotic state of perpetual positivity. Meanwhile, the harsh and discordant notes and backbeats of racism and discrimination have been kept from our consciousness, drowned out by far happier melodies.[18]

Racial prejudice and discrimination is a part of life for people in the inner-city. It has become so natural that in many instances, it does not hurt anymore, but still generates anger. Jail, incarceration, or even death is just another form of escape. "Today blatant, subtle, and covert discrimination against African Americans persists in virtually all aspects of their public life. Racial discrimination is pervasive and cumulative and costly in its impact."[19] The inner-city mind is crucified with the knowledge and experience of injustice and inequality. The inner-city mind is insulted by the placating scriptural references of the conversion gospel that speaks to the "next world" while living in hell here on earth. The inner-city mind remembers that it was evangelicals that owned slaves and perpetuated an initial chattel system of human trafficking. "The sheer absurdity that confronts human beings of African descent in this country,

18. Wise, *Dear White America*, 104.
19. Feagin and Sikes, *Living with Racism,* 319.

the incessant assaults on black intelligence, beauty, character, and possibility."[20] The inner-city mind is searching for answers to the social sin of racism but is not finding an aggressive rhetoric to satisfy the oppression of inequality. The media is not making this search an easy one in that it will be sure to broadcast this injustice directly into the homes of inner-city black and brown people.

As a consequence, the evangelical inner-city mind is torn between the dichotomies of theory and practice. There seems to be no remedy to the theological pathology of what is believed and what is practiced. Racism in the eyes of the inner-city becomes the vision of what they see in the eyes of white America and the system that enslaved them. How can one be in Christ, but not of Christ? How can Jesus Christ be the object of our worship, but the fault of our individuality? Who answers the question, "O wretched man that I am! Who shall deliver me from this body of this death?" (Rom 7:24). Emerson and Smith argue two opposing points in how to answer this question:

> First, attempts at corrective action, perhaps by black Christians, may be countered by white evangelicals because such action simply seems wrong from their vantage point. To the extent that overcoming racialization depend in part on social programs and policies, evangelicals' general opposition to such programs and policies perhaps serves to heighten racialization. Why? Second, White evangelicals' cultural tools and racial isolation direct them to see the world individualistically and as a series of discrete incidents. They also direct them to desire a color-blind society. Black evangelicals tend to see the racial world very differently. Ironically, evangelicalism's cultural tools lead people in different social and geographical realities to access the race problem in divergent and non-reconciliatory ways. This large gulf in understanding is perhaps part of the race problem's core, and most certainly contributes to the entrenchment of the racialized society.[21]

20. West, *Race Matters*, 95.

21. Emerson and Smith, *Divided by Faith* 90–91.

Cone gives a powerful comparative imagery with the lynching of black people and the Cross of Jesus Christ. He utilizes the dichotomies of the Cross and the lynching tree as realities faced by black people in their search for a theological hope of deliverance through the Cross of Christ and the holocaustic reality of their life and death survival while surviving in the American way. The similarity of Jesus' blood on the cross to lead the captives free is more than coincidental to the blood black people shed on the trees of Southern racism in that same endeavor: freedom. "I believe that the cross placed alongside the lynching tree can help us to see Jesus in America in a new light, and thereby empower people who claim to follow him to take a stand against white supremacy and every kind of injustice."[22] The paradoxical relationship of the Cross of Christ and the lynching tree of black people brings into conversation the purpose of each.

The Cross of Christ brought life to all those who believed in the sanctity of the sacrificial blood He shed. The good news of the crucifixion is not the death of Christ, but the resurrection victory over that death. Life for all came as the result of the death of one. On the other hand, the lynching tree brought death to over 5,000 black people, and their deaths symbolized the resurrection victory over the injustices that threatened generations of other blacks with the same fate. The lynching tree is not a symbol of death and defeat, but is a symbol of the evil perpetuated upon the minds of a people who refused to allow it to overshadow the grace of God to overcome sin and death. The passion of Christ became the saving grace for His people. The action of the cross brought a relational cohesiveness of mysterious experience with the Son of God. "In the mystery of God's revelation, black Christians believed that just knowing that Jesus went through an experience of suffering in a manner similar to theirs gave them faith that God was with them, even in suffering on lynching trees, just as God was present with Jesus in suffering on the cross."[23]

22. Cone, *The Cross and The Lynching Tree*, xix.
23. Ibid., 22.

The historical coincidences of the time of Christ and the times of racial murder in the South deserve more than a casual examination. Looking through the lens of James Cone and Black Theology, the historical context of lynching illustrates a perceived prophetic outcome as a result of "sin taking its course." A brief examination of the table below demonstrates a few particular similarities.

## Comparison of the Cross and the Lynching Tree

| Jesus and the Cross | Blacks and the Lynching Tree |
| --- | --- |
| Jesus was the victim of mob violence | Blacks were targets |
| Jesus was killed in the name of God | Blacks were killed in the name of God |
| The cross was a symbol of terror, torture and execution, reserved for criminals, slaves and insurrectionists | The lynching tree was a symbol of terror, torture and execution, reserved for slaves and insurrectionists |
| Jesus was publically humiliated | Blacks were publically humiliated |
| Crucifixion was a public spectacle | Lynching was a public affair |
| Jesus was stripped, mocked and whipped, pierced, spat upon | Blacks were stripped, mocked, castrated, whipped, pierced, spat upon |
| Christians, women and men, were burned upon crosses | Blacks, women and men were burned sometime as they hung from the tree |
| Jesus thought the Father had forsaken him | Blacks believed the Father had forsaken them |
| The purpose of the cross was to strike terror in people—to keep them in their place | The purpose of the lynching tree was to strike terror in people—to keep blacks in their place |

When an examination of the "lynching trees" located in the inner-city are revealed; many black and brown people are hanging from trees of poverty, lack of a quality education, unemployment, violence, mass incarceration, crime, over-policing, injustice, isolation, and apathetic churches. Cone argues:

> Black Churches are also guilty of prostituting the name of God's church. The black denominational churches seem to be content with things as they are, getting fat on the misery of their sisters and brothers. The black churches satisfy themselves with white solutions to earthly injustice. That is why persons interested in justice in this world so often scorn the black church, saying that it is nothing but a second-rate oppressor.[24]

The result of these inner-city "lynching trees" is precious blood upon the streets of poor neighborhoods from victim's survival at the cost of salvation. The arbitrary violence that flows in and through the inner-city streets is just another experience and reminder of the blood of the Cross of Christ. "When blacks sang about the "blood," they were wrestling not only with the blood of the crucified carpenter from Nazareth but also with the blood of raped and castrated black bodies in America—innocent, often nameless, burning and hanging bodies, images of hurt so deep that only God's 'amazing grace' could offer consolation."[25]

Cone reminds us that there is a symbiotic relationship between the cross and the lynching tree. The depth of this relationship is fully realized each Sunday morning. In the traditional worship services of the black church, mothers cry for the lives of those who have hung from inner-city lynching trees and even more tears are shed for the lives of those they hope will never see the rope of injustice and hatred that, like a snare, tightens around their neck as they struggle for their freedom. "The cross needs the lynching tree to remind Americans of the reality of suffering-to keep the cross from becoming a symbol of abstract, sentimental piety. Yet the lynching tree also needs the cross. It is the cross that points in the direction of hope, the confidence that there is a dimension to life beyond the reach of the oppressor."[26] The cross is the hope and

24 Cone, *A Black Theology of Liberation*, 134.

25. Cone, *The Cross and the Lynching Tree*, 75.

26. Ibid., 163.

symbol of Christianity and the lynching tree is the result and symbol of black suffering; but through it all Cone offers his perspective of hope between the two.

Cone reminds us:

> No gulf between blacks and whites is too great to overcome, for our beauty is more enduring than our brutality. The lynching tree is a metaphor for white America's crucifixion of black people. In this sense, black people are Christ figures, not because they wanted to suffer but because they had no choice. God took the evil of the cross and the lynching tree and transformed them both into the triumphant beauty of the divine. If America has the courage to confront the great sin and ongoing legacy of white supremacy with repentance and reparation, there is hope "beyond tragedy."[27]

27. Cone, *The Cross and the Lynching Tree*, 166.

# CHAPTER 8

# The New Face of Systematic Racism

*The Theological Implications for Inner-City*
*Ministry*

*"I pledge allegiance to the flag of the United States of America and*
*to the republic for which as stands, one nation under God, indivisible*
*with liberty and justice for all."*

EVERY PERSON WHO RECITES this pledge promises to be loyal to
the symbol of our country and affirms that each state has joined
as a republic where people choose others to make laws for them.
The flag represents this country; one nation united under the
supervision and direction of one God with freedom and fairness
for each person in the country. Richard J. Ellis gives a comprehensive history of the pledge of allegiance and the meaning to the
people of this country. The colors of the flag were carefully chosen
to represent the history of this country since its beginning: white
signifies purity and innocence, red, hardness and valor, and blue,
the color of vigilance, perseverance and justice, while every star
represents each state joined in agreement with this pledge. Created
by a Baptist minister and Christian Socialist, Frances Bellamy, the
original history of the pledge of allegiance is one carefully formed
with government control even as people say it proudly with illu-
sions of freedom blinding them from the reality that we are all
slaves to a worldly autocratic authority. The term "under God"

(added later to the pledge) from its inception into the pledge mirrored a history that America, unlike communist nations, is a religious nation. Richard J. Ellis states:

> A letter sent by the Bush White House to those writing the president regarding the Ninth Circuit's decision amplified Bush's understanding of the meaning of the "under God" clause. The letter, issued over Bush's signature, reiterated the president's belief that the Pledge helped "define our Nation" and that the Pledge affirmed "our reliance on God." When we pledge allegiance to One Nation under God, our citizens participate in an important American tradition of humbly seeking the wisdom and blessing of Divine Providence.[1]

In the minds of other American Presidents, including; Bush, Woodrow Wilson and Ronald Reagan, the United States is a nation set aside by God to lead other nations in America's divine mission to be united together by a set of universal values and to be nurtured by those values. However, the ambiguity of a one nation "under God" conflicts with a religious conception understood by Black Theology. Ellis goes on to argue that,

> Bush's answer underscores the ways in which a religious conception of national identity excludes those who do not share that religious belief, just as surely as a racial or ethnic conception of national identity excludes those not of that race or ethnicity. Little wonder that the Pledge's declaration that the United States is "one nation under God" appears to atheists to be logically akin to the statement that the United States is "one nation under white males"—historically accurate perhaps, but exclusionary nonetheless.[2]

As an institution, slavery represented much of what can be compared to our present day incarceration prison system. The analogy of the institution of slavery and the present prison system with an end result of segregation and racism are like an illicit relationship

1. Ellis, *To the Flag,* 217.
2. Ibid., 219.

that binds its participants as strange bedfellows. Martin Luther King Jr., stated, "Segregation is the adultery of an illicit intercourse between injustice and immorality." A new Jim Crow sleeps with a mistress of mass incarceration in the motel of institutional systems that operate collectively to pimp a large group of people is an immoral un-holy covenant that profits America in the hallways of justice.

To further the argument about the relationship between injustice (mass incarceration) and immorality (Jim Crow/slavery), certain parallels between the two are strikingly similar when an examination of the two are visualized in the context of the inner-city. Those parallels include historical, legalized discrimination, political disenfranchisement, exclusive from juries, a closed court system to those of color, and a symbolic production of life through media stereotypic images. There is a declared and undeclared war on the black and brown youth of our inner-cities. These wars have legitimized the taking of inner-city prisoners and confining them in prison plantations as the "new slave." The declared war is the War on Drugs policy of 1973 and the continued undeclared war takes place in the media and its attack on the inner-city.

The War on Drugs has as its focus point, "Convictions for drug offenses are the single most important cause of the explosion incarceration rates in the United States."[3] This declared war has profound effect on black and brown youth in the inner-city context. The explosion of incarceration oppression was not an instantaneous occurrence, but in fact has been developing for quite a few years. The ages of those who fall to this system are from within the hip-hop generation. It imprisons many young men at a point in their lives where they are transitioning from boyhood into manhood. Drug arrests have tripled since 1980, and as a result, more than 31 million people have been arrested for drug offenses since the drug war began according to Marc Mauer.[4]

Within the inner-city community, rumors of "conspiracy" abound and are no longer whispered in passing anger or indignation.

3. Ibid., 60.
4. Mauer and King, *A 25-Year Quagmire*, 2.

One such rumor says that if the government wanted to stop drugs in the inner-city it would but does not because the government is a bigger "dope man" than the gang-banger that stands on the corner. There is another rumor that the military like weaponry that found its way into the hands of gang-bangers also came from the government and that the "plan" of the government is to eventually wipe out all black and brown youth or at least have them segregated in such a way they cannot make a significant contribution to society; that is, they will be caught up in a cycle of incarceration and control which takes them out of the American way of life. The word, 'genocide' comes to mind. The Urban League came to take the claims of genocide seriously. In its 1990 report "The State of Black America," it stated: "There is at least one concept that must be recognized if one is to see the pervasive and insidious nature of the drug problem for the African American community. Though difficult to accept, that is the concept of genocide."[5] There have been several accounts about an admission of CIA involvement in the drug trade that affected black neighborhoods:

> The CIA admitted in 1998 that guerrilla armies it actively supported in Nicaragua were smuggling illegal drugs into the United States—drugs that were making their way onto the streets of inner-city black neighborhoods in the form of crack cocaine. The CIA also admitted that, in the midst of the War on Drugs, it blocked law enforcement efforts to investigate illegal drug networks that were helping to fund its covert war in Nicaragua.[6]

There is yet another rumor that fuels the assumption that crack cocaine is a "black" drug, and that it is at the bottom of the problems suffered by the inner-city. The War on Drugs is a good thing because it is designed to put high profile drug dealers in jail and in this effort eliminate an evil that oppresses people. It is the drugs and not the political structures that are oppressive. It is because black and brown people make a choice to do drugs and

5. Page, "'The Plan': A Paranoid View of Black Problems," 212-13.
6. Cockburn and St. Clair, *Whiteout: The CIA, Drugs, and the Press.*

break the law; and hip-hop rap glorifies the usage of crack. Jeffrey O. G. Ogbar observes:

> The rapid expansion of the prison industrial complex has been a salient feature of hip-hop narratives since the 1980's. The earliest references to prisons in hip-hop emerged simultaneously with the initial rapid expansion of the prison industry in the late 1980's. The rise was co-terminous with the crack scourge that swept the country resulting in a spiraling murder rate and a sharp rise in other violent crimes.[7]

Ogbar argues that the Presidential administrations of Reagan and the George H. W. Bush actually endorsed increasing prisons as a means of control to a fast growing crime rate to maintain the conservative spirit of "law and order." Prisons, like the War on Drugs, are necessary to control the criminal elements found on the streets of this country to secure the safety of the public and ensure a greater good in the process. Other scholars have also agreed and documented the argument presented by Ogbar. The War on Drugs was an erroneous presumption of the government to take back the streets of the inner-city which has lost its way due to the crack epidemic; however, the fact is that crack was not an issue in the inner-city before the declaration of war.

The War on Drugs then took an economical up-turn for the wealthy elite. A mile stone amendment to the Comprehensive Drug Abuse Prevention and Control Act (1978) now allows law enforcement to seize all money and/or other things of value furnished or intended to be furnished by any person in exchange for a controlled substance and all proceeds traceable to such an exchange. In other words, it was now "finders' keepers, losers' weepers" for drug agencies who kept the proceeds from all illegal drug deals no matter how large or small. "Every system of control depends for its survival on the tangible and intangible benefits that are provided to those who are responsible for the system's maintenance and administration."[8] In other words, what Alexander is de-

7. Ogbar, *Hip-Hop Revolution,* 139.
8. Ibid., 72.

scribing here is that money is needed to support every war. Besides the blatant federal support of the war, policies prove that federal dollars financed local street level soldiers of this war (policing).

The Byrne program, named after a fallen police officer, was designed to encourage every federal grant recipient to help fight the War on Drugs (see table below). Millions of dollars in federal aid have been offered to state and local law enforcement agencies willing to wage the war. Alexander argues that these financial incentives encouraged local agencies to pump up their drug arrests with little publicity, leading the general public to believe the drug problem has doubled or tripled in a short time, and that these arrests reflect a surge in illegal drug activity rather than an infusion of money and an intensified enforcement effort. It is about the money; the system needs to be fed. The table below illustrates the financial distribution of the money required to support the systematic equipping of war artillery in the inner-city.

Consequently, an ironic conflict of interest exists. There is a double-mindedness, at least minimally, in receiving the disbursements. Jimmie Reeves and Richard Campbell suggest a "double-bind." A conflict of interest exists in the form that those responsible for fighting the drug war and bringing it to a conclusive end are also caught up with wanting it to continue because they are financially rewarded for their participation in the very war they are sworn to end.

## Distribution by Percentages of the Byrne JAG Formula Grant in California in 2009

| Byrne JAG purpose area | Dollar Amount | Percent of Total |
| --- | --- | --- |
| Law Enforcement | 65,263,716 | 38.87% |
| Prosecution & Courts | 10,000,000 | 5.96% |
| Prevention & Education | 1,140,000 | 0.68% |

| Byrne JAG purpose area | Dollar Amount | Percent of Total |
| --- | --- | --- |
| Corrections & Community Corrections | 45,000,000 | 26.80% |
| Drug Treatment & Enforcement | 45,000,000 | 26.80% |
| Planning, Evaluation & Technology | 0 | 0.00% |
| Crime Victim & Witness | 1,500,000 | 0.89% |
| Total | 167,903,716 | 100.00% |

Note. This includes Recovery Act and any other Byrne JAG funding allocated from the FY2009 or earlier awards. (Not included in these data are the $20,989,630 in direct grants awarded directly by DOJ/Bureau of Justice Assistance to 276 counties and municipalities in California under the FY2009 appropriations bill, and the $89,712,677 awarded to 420 localities under the Recovery Act). Source: http://www.ncjp.org/states/ca?vdt=glossary%7Cpage_2.

Penal economic prosperity is experienced at the prison level also in what Angela Davis describes as an industrial prison complex. "This massive imprisonment arose as a convenient response of first resort to far too many of the social problems that burden people who are ensconced in poverty. Once this happens, mass imprisonment of people in the oppressed communities literally become[s] big business."[9] On the street level of the inner-city, the definition is understood that the prison industrial complex is a system that brings government and business together and uses prisons as a solution to social, political and economic problems. It is made up of police, courts, the media and any other organization that does not want to hear the voice of black and brown people. In other words, the prison industrial complex is just another way the government and corporations are messing America up. Bakari Kitwana suggests:

9. Davis, *Masked Racism,* 683.

Those incarcerated in the United States is quickly approaching 2 million, at this point the private sector in prison housing and labor is only scratching the surface. In some cases, lawmakers at federal and state levels have given the nod to policies that could eventually make the prison industrial complex a reality. At most, what we have today is a foundation for what could become a prison industrial complex. The inroads that have been made in privatizing the prison industry have created a profit motive for keeping young blacks locked up.[10]

There is a prison industrial complex operating here in America. When an examination of the statistics presented above is considered, it can be easily deduced why and how companies like Corrections Corporations of America (CCA), Geo Group, and Management and Training Corporation now exist. Part of the agreement between these companies and the states in which they operate is that the state is responsible for the occupancy requirements. That is, these privatized prisons will demand the state to keep at least ninety percent full at all times whether crime was rising or falling. In order for this demand to be satisfied per the contract, advertising of stigma and stereotypes by the media is important.

Malcolm X revealed the power of the media to shape the hearts and minds of the people when he stated, "The media's the most powerful entity on earth. They have the power to make the innocent guilty and make the guilty innocent, and that's power. Because of the control of the minds of the masses." This statement becomes very important when it is understood how the media has and continues to play a major role with the images of discrimination. It can be argued that without the images of discrimination, most people would not know what it looks like; however, when an image of discrimination is seen, the responsibility of what to do after seeing it becomes a matter of conviction. The War on Drugs became a political and media event. When myopic vision is peeking through a crack all one sees are crack images; "crack

10. Kitwana, *The Hip-Hop Generation*, 75.

whores," "crack babies," and "crack dealers." Each of these images are painted black in the public eye through local media.

There is a psychology behind the media advertising of discrimination and race that continues to perpetuate the hatred of a race of people that many white Americans do not know. In other words, faith is no greater than what is seen and what is seen becomes reality. In a recent study conducted by Birt L. Duncan, a group of whites were shown a video in which two men, one black and one white, were arguing. When the white man (who was an actor) shoved the black man at the end of the argument, only seventeen percent of whites viewing the incident said they perceived the act as violent; but when the black actor administered the shove, three of four whites said they perceived the act as a violent one.[11]

In order to outline the dimensions of this war, two things were important: First identify the enemy and second determine the battle ground. In order to make these two things clear in the eyes of America, network television news media was deployed. David Jerigan and Lori Dorfman conducted a study of network television news from 1990 through 1991 and found that a predictable "us against them" frame was used in the news stories, with "us" being white, suburban America, and "them" being black Americans and a few corrupted whites.[12] Presently, the image of the black "criminal" is perpetuated with images of saggy pants, certain colors, black men with hoodies, tattoos, and bald heads, identifying them as the "enemy." News coverage of violent street crimes most typically interview black or brown people who confirm this imagery with code words like "gang related," or "the suspect was a black man," or from in "South Central Los Angeles," even though they may be standing in a place not considered to even be in Los Angeles County. Jerome Miller, the former executive director of the National Center for Institutions and Alternatives stated, "There are certain code words that allow you never to have to say 'race,' but

11. Duncan, "Differential Social Perception and Attributes of Intergroup Violence: Testing the Lower Limits of Stereotyping of Blacks,"

12. Jerigan and Dorfman, "Visualizing America's Drug Problems: An Ethnographic Content Analysis of Illegal Drug Stories," 169, 188.

everybody knows that's what you mean and 'crime' is one of those. So when we talk about locking up more and more people, what we are really talking about is locking up more and more black men."[13]

Now that the battle grounds and enemies have been identified, the political justification and allies for this war are solidified. Jimmie Reeves and Richard Campbell make this claim:

> In challenging the counterfeit claims underwriting Reagan's war on drugs. . .we believe it is much more productive to focus on how the "behaviorist" orientation of drug control experts and the "individualist" orientation of mainstream journalists were co-opted by the "moralist" crusaders of the New Right during the Reagan era. Ultimately, this is the central charge that we set out to prove in this book-a charge that connects news coverage of the war on drugs to the "new racism," the "family values," and the "orthodoxy of nostalgia" of the Reagan counterrevolution.[14]

There is still yet another war that has claimed the right to legitimizing black prisoners: The War on Poverty. The War on Poverty is directly related to the low economic status of inner-city streets and contributes itself to self-serving social conditions that perpetuate the poverty. However, the War on Poverty did not take as many prisoners as classically designed; therefore, the War on Drugs became the greatest battle for that purpose. "Thus it is here, in the poverty stricken, racially segregated ghettos, where the War on Poverty has been abandoned and factories have disappeared, that the drug war has been waged with the greatest ferocity."[15]

At the height of the crack cocaine epidemic, a recession was hitting this country. During the 1980's many people were hit with economic challenges, but none as severe was what was happening in the inner-city. With the advent of globalization and American blue collar jobs going over-seas to foreign countries, combined

13. Szykowny, "No Justice, No Peace: An Interview with Jerome Miller," 9-19.

14. Reeves and Campbell, *Cracked Coverage*, 2.

15. Alexander, *The New Jim Crow*, 124.

with new advances in technology the classic jobs (such as automotive, defense, and construction), and the phenomenon of "white flight" to the suburbs, the inner-city is quickly becoming a wilderness of joblessness. Without the proper education (unavailable in the inner-city school systems), adequate training, and proper levels of computer based operations in street level commerce, jobs opportunities for black and brown people seem bleak. As William Julius Wilson indicates, those residing in ghetto communities were particularly ill equipped to adapt to the seismic changes taking place in the American economy. By 1987, when the drug war hit high gear, the industrial employment of black men and women had plummeted to 28 percent.[16]

The loss of employment opportunities in the inner-cities and the lucrative pull of the drug trade "set-up" the taking of black and brown prisoners in the drug war. Additionally, media depiction of this "choice" deliberately makes it seem like the inner-city is a benefactor rather than a victim of this dilemma. Upon further investigation, when the media uses images of black and brown women as the "face" and chief recipients of welfare, poverty is shown with the wrong perspective. Just as black and brown men are made the target as criminals and drug dealers of the War on Drugs, conversely, black and brown women are targeted as lazy and unmotivated to get jobs and get off welfare. "The (alleged) misbehaviors of the poor were transformed from adaptations to poverty that had the unfortunate effect of reproducing it into character failings that accounted for poverty in the first place. Black "welfare cheats" and their dangerous offspring emerged, for the first time, in the political discourse and media imagery."[17]

The media continues to exert it power in the minds of conservative Americans as it was used as a weapon to capture the minds of voters who are torn between the conviction to intervene in poverty of blacks and those who believe that poverty, crime, and unemployment are just devices of manipulation of black culture to get more "governmental handouts."

16. Wilson, *When Work Disappears*, 31.
17. Beckett, *Making Crime Pay*, 34.

The hip-hop generation visualizes their lives completely different than what racialized society has forced them to be. Many young hip-hoppers who have not been able to take advantage of a good education, a two- parent home, a good job, and freedom of movement do not see that a "regular" job offers them any redemption. The drug dealers who are "making it" always seem to have money and are willing to assist the young "g's" with a street knowledge that has adapted to the hand dealt them. "In the 1980s and 1990s, many hip-hop generationers quickly realized that a forty-hour-a-week, minimum-wage job would not meet their basic needs. That many of us would take our chances in the informal economy is not surprising hence the mass appeal enjoyed by rap lyrics that described a gritty underworld."[18]

What are the implications of the new face of systematic racism on inner-city ministry? How do we minister to young people who are frustrated with how things are and will not be satisfied with how things will become? What does all this have to do with theology? At this point, it must be understood that a new rhetoric must be spoken to a new generation. One of the ingredients of the Willie Lynch letter is "controlled language." A portion of the letter states, "You know language is a peculiar institution. It leads to the heart of a people. So you have to be careful in setting up the new language; for the slaves would soon be in your house, talking to you as "man to man" and that is death to our economic system." The questions must be answered with a new rhetoric that aggressively answers in a manner relevant to the present day. Those answers may not come from traditional Christian preaching and may be outside the pages of "thee" and "thou" of the King James Bible. Cone makes this distinction:

> I did not have the time to do the theological and historical research needed to present a "balanced" perspective on the problem of racism in America. Black men, women, and children were being shot and imprisoned for asserting their right to a dignified existence. Others were wasting away in ghettos, dying from filth, rats, and

18. Kitwana, *The Hip-Hop Generation,* 35.

dope, as white and black ministers preached about a blond, blue-eyed Jesus who came to make us all just like him. I had to speak a different word, not just as a black person but primarily as a theologian.[19]

The implications for the new face of systemic racism will have several levels that must be considered as an attempt is made to answer the first question. First of all, the rhetoric must not be in the tone of understanding, nor can it be rhetoric of separate but equal. Separate but equal is what created the mistrust and anger still present in the inner-city. In other words, the church must stand as a single voice with a righteous indignation against an evil that has persisted so long in America. Emerson and Smith have identified four levels of racial practices that continue racial division in America. The plan of the church should be to systematically eliminate those divisions. These divisions are identified as being: (1) Increasingly covert, (2) Embedded in normal operations of institutions, (3) Formed to avoid direct racial terminology, and (4) Invisible to most whites.[20] Racism and discrimination in all the social institutions must be identified and eliminated. As a result, racism is not an individual evil, but a systemic misuse of power that results in diminished life opportunities for some racial groups. Consequently, the church must open the rhetoric of exposure from within rather from without.

When religion is viewed sociologically its definitive role changes; "Religion is a set of beliefs and practices focused on the sacred or supernatural, through which life experiences of groups and individuals are given meaning and direction by providing significance and purpose to life as it is, religion provides legitimization for the world as it is."[21] Religion thought of in this manner means that the focus of sacred faith cannot be in the over yonder alone; it must be couched in how religion communicates the rhetoric of salvation in the here and now. The narrow view of religion is that it is a sustainer of the status quo. Emerson and Smith argue that

19. Cone, *A Black Theology of Liberation, Twentieth ed.*, xii.

20. Emerson and Smith, *Divided by Faith*, 9.

21. Ibid., 17.

evangelicals usually fail to challenge the system not just out of concern for evangelism, but also because they support the American system and enjoy its fruits and it is sometimes a failure to evaluate whether the social system is consistent with their Christianity.[22]

Black Theology and traditional Christian theology must have the same rhetoric spoken with the same passion of dissatisfaction about the social normality of racism. Racism and injustice have been so much a part of the inner-city it has become a way of life; inner-city life does not work through but along-side of racism as a neighbor that lives next door. The mandate of Black Theology is to set people free from the things that oppress them. "Evangelism historically meant freeing black folks' souls from sin and their bodies from physical, political, and social oppression, and of setting the conditions of existence so that they could achieve full humanity. It is for them a special call from God thrust upon them that was different from that of their white counterparts."[23]

How does the church minister to young people who are frustrated with how things are and will not be satisfied with how things will become? A mind cannot be free if it is locked in a body that is imprisoned. The social pathologies of inner-city life must be minimized politically as justice is maximized spiritually. The conjugality of Black Theology and Holy Hip-hop will bring a forceful rhetoric of reconciliation sung in the genre of hip-hop. The conscience rap of hip-hop in conjunction with the focus of Black Theology demands justice and equality for all people. Otis Moss III speaks to this language of societal injustices through hip-hop:

> Hip hop uses language and technology to entertain, critique, and define the urban centers from which it originates. Hip hop is a means for young black men and women to define their reality. It gives value to their world, which has been defined by white culture as having no value. It may not always be positive or Afrocentric, but hip hop points to the problems in society that many black people have refused to address. The hip hop

22. Ibid. 22.
23. Stallings, *Telling the Story*, 20.

community recognizes the contradiction of urban existence and the fallacy of the American dream founded upon a system that exploits people of color.[24]

Finally, whether it is understood that its Black Theology, traditional Christian theology, or the theology of Holy Hip-hop, the church has a large responsibility. As one whole body united as members of that body, the church must speak to the mountain by faith. Emerson and Smith say it best:

> Within the very forces able to render religion a legitimator of the world are revolutionary impulses able to change the world. Because religion is oriented not toward the mundane but toward the sacred or supernatural, it establishes a perceived objective reality above and beyond space and time. The seeds of change are planted in the faith. In this way, the ultimate legitimator of the status quo can easily become its ultimate judge. This dual potential lies precisely in the ultimacy [sic] and distance that characterizes sacred transcendence itself. Emboldened by the sacred, religion can be a powerful source for change.[25]

Only when the church takes it rightful place as the conscience of this nation can the citizens that live within its borders can say with hesitation: *I pledge allegiance to the flag of the United States of America and to the republic for which as stands, one nation **under God**, indivisible with liberty and justice for all.*

---

24. Moss, "Real Big," 114.
25. Emerson and Smith, *Divided by Faith*, 18.

# CHAPTER 9

# The Stockholm Syndrome of Religious Thought

THERE ARE CIRCUMSTANCES BEYOND the control or the auspices of the local church. However, when these circumstances are collectively a hindrance to the Body of Christ, it would seem appropriate that the church aggressively attack the circumstance. Historically, the church has always been the place of social reform, social advocacy, and shelter from oppression. Recently, that position has eroded away by complacency, withdrawal, or silence. When it appears that the church has turned its ecclesiastical back on those who depend on it for guidance, the structure of the Body of Christ breaks down. These social pathologies as they affect the Body of Christ have been termed by Martin Luther King Jr., as "midnight." In the inner-city particularly, there are two types of black churches; although the term black is used, these kinds of churches can be of any ethnicity. Each of these types of churches will respond differently when the "midnight" of poor education, poverty, lack of employment, and over policing becomes the "midnight."

> Two types of Negro churches have failed to provide bread. One burns with emotionalism, and the other freezes with classism. The former reducing worship to entertainment, places more emphasis on volume than on content and confuses spirituality with muscularity. The danger in such a church is that the members may have more religion in their hands and feet than in their hearts

and souls. At midnight this type of church has neither the vitality nor the relevant gospel to feed hungry souls.[1]

The church that screams of emotional witness sets the stage for the words of the preacher who uses this platform as an audition for his own glory and fame. It is this type of church that will give itself over to an over-rationalization of the midnight, but will not suggest any type of resolve because it is powerless in all things except its charismatic leader.

The other church type is one of pious stardom. This church is one where the front seats are reserved for the greatest tither or giver. It is a place where the center of worship turns from the altar of God to the celebrity in the pews.

> The other type of Negro church that feeds no midnight traveler has developed a class system and boasts of its dignity, its membership of professional people, and its exclusiveness. In such a church the worship service is cold and meaningless, the music dull and uninspiring, and the sermon little more than a homily on current events. If the pastor says too much about Jesus Christ, the members feel that he is robbing the pulpit of dignity. If the choir sings a Negro spiritual, the members claim an affront to their class status. This type of church tragically fails to recognize that worship at is best is a social experience in which people from all levels of life come together to affirm their oneness and unity under God. At midnight men are altogether ignored because their limited education or they are given bread that has been hardened by the winger of morbid class consciousness.[2]

Cone argues these types of churches must repent. He argues that theology is always done for particular times and places and addresses a specific audience. He admits that although God is the intended subject of theology, God does not do theology; human beings do theology. He tries to uncover the "wrongheadedness" of the white way of doing theology and then attempts to set Christian

1  King, *Strength to Love*, 60.

2.  Ibid., 60.

theology on the right path of liberation. Within the context of the inner-city, it is important Christian theology is concerned with a holistic application to daily life, the here and now of faith. If faith comes to the poor by hearing, then the rhetoric spoken must be from the context of the poor; if faith comes to the oppressed by hearing, then the rhetoric must be spoken from the context of oppression. "There is no way that a church or institution can be related to the gospel of Christ if it sponsors or tolerates racism in any form. To speak of a "racist Christian" or a "segregated church of Christ" is blasphemy and the antithesis of the Christian gospel."[3]

The Stockholm syndrome is simply defined as the psychological tendency of a hostage to bond with, identify with, or sympathize with his or her captor. The origin of this phenomenon came from a 1973 robbery attempt in Stockholm, Sweden, during which bank employees held hostage developed sympathetic feelings toward their captors. Joseph M. Carver, Ph.D., and noted Clinical Psychologist noted the following:

> It has been found that four situations or conditions are present that serve as a foundation for the development of Stockholm Syndrome. These four situations can be found in hostage, severe abuse, and abusive relationships: (1) The presence of a perceived threat to one's physical or psychological survival and the belief that the abuser would carry out the threat. (2) The presence of a perceived small kindness from the abuser to the victim (3) Isolation from perspectives other than those of the abuser (4) The perceived inability to escape the situation.[4]

There is still yet another connection of the Stockholm syndrome that must be considered when examined in line with religious thought. The theory of "Cognitive Dissonance" explains how and why people change their ideas and opinions to support situations that do not appear to be healthy or normal. In other words, an individual seeks to reduce information or opinions that make him or her uncomfortable. Leon Festinger, an influential figure

3. Cone, *A Black Theology of Liberation*, 14.
4. Carver, "Love and Stockholm Syndrome," 1.

in social psychology, developed the foundations for this theory which is based on a simple premise: human beings do not like inconsistency. Inconsistency agitates human beings to the point that the greater the inconsistency, the more motivation to reduce that inconsistency. Joel M. Cooper makes this summation:

> The state of cognitive dissonance occurs when people believe that two of their psychological representations are inconsistent with each other. More formally, a pair of cognitions is inconsistent if one cognition follows from the obverse (opposite) of the other. An example will help: A person believes that he should give money to the poor but he passes by an indigent person on the street without contributing money to the man's cup. These two cognitions are dissonant because not giving money follows from the obverse of his belief. Not giving money follows logically from a belief that one should not contribute to the poor. But, in our example, the person held a belief that did not coincide with his behavior. We can say that the two cognitions were inconsistent or dissonant with each other. Or: *If a person holds cognitions A and B such that A follows from the opposite of B, then A and B are dissonant.*[5]

Arguably, people involved making a difficult decision showed favor toward the chosen alternative considerably more, and the rejected alternative significantly less than they had rated the same alternatives prior to the choice. Cooper argues a conclusion based on the work of another sociologist, Jack Brehm, introducing what has been established as the free choice paradigm. The free choice paradigm suggests three conclusions about cognitive dissonance: First, cognitive dissonance occurs following decisions, and second, it is reduced by attitude change that spreads the attractiveness of the choice alternatives. In other words, the chosen alternative becomes more attractive; the un-chosen alternative becomes less attractive. Lastly, Cooper argues that the more difficult the decision, the greater the dissonance.[6]

5. Cooper, *Cognitive Dissonance*, 6.

6 Cooper, *Cognitive Dissonance*, 14.

Ethically speaking, the church is faced with a plethora of decisions/choices that has forced it to be held captive to the culture which surrounds it. In the midst of that captivity, the church has acculturated and sympathized with its captor. The cognitive dissonance of denominations has transformed the religious principles of Jesus Christ into a survival consumerist thinking of big organizational business operations. In the churches effort not to be confirmed to this world, it begins to look more and more like the world. There are Christian television shows that mimic the talent competitions of American Idol and game shows with a biblical format that resemble secular game shows.

Christian leaders who are supposed to be shepherds of the sheep of Christ have begun to compare themselves with the lifestyles of hip-hop rappers. From the inner-city perspective, racism exists just as deeply in the church as it does in the world. Martin Luther King Jr., in his Letter from a Birmingham Jail states, "The church was not merely a thermometer that recorded the ideas and principles of popular opinion, it was a thermostat that transformed the mores of society."[7] The silence of the church in the midst of systemic racism makes it hostage to, in bond with, identified with, and a sympathizer with an oppressor.

It becomes apparent that in light of the cognitive dissonance argument that an examination of church position in relation to race is important to locate. The example cited above in the quotation by Cooper illustrates the dichotomy between practice and theory. If scripture confirms that the poor are to be fed but the church does not; if scripture confirms that it is to seek and save the lost but the church does not; if scripture confirms that the church is to free the captives but it does not; if scripture confirms believers are to love one another as themselves but does not, then the argument of cognitive dissonance is confirmed in the non-activities of the church. In other words, according to the argument of cognitive dissonance the church is not being consistent in doing what the church believes, therefore the following applies: *If the church holds cognitions A (racism is evil) and B (racism should not be tolerated by*

7. Gilbreath, *Birmingham Revolution*, 39.

*the church) such that the evil of racism (A) follows from the opposite of racism should not be tolerated by the church (B), then A (the evil of racism) should not be tolerated by the church (B) are dissonant.*

The inappropriate church practice of thinking that church is a geographic location, a street address, or particular denomination is scripturally an opprobrium upon the principles of the Cross. "Without prophetic self-criticism, churches become self-serving institutions for their ministers, officers, and members, and theology, without Christian community as the place of its origin and its continued existence, becomes sterile academic discourse uninterested in the quality of human life in society."[8] Prideful self-minded thinking causes believers in the church to say, "Not my church" or "His church is not like that" or "Their church could do more" takes away from the community of what *the church* should be doing. This type of cognitive dissonance is particularly abrasive in the inner-city context. When the church is examined as a whole, it seems irrelevant, uninterested in the welfare of others, and at best blind with its head in the sand. From an inner-city perspective, that position shows nothing of the church but its backside.

It is also offensive to see the divisive theologies of white church and black church; the black church that preaches a social gospel as the white church continues to preach individualism and status quo salvation. These labels have been necessary to understand the intricacies involved with the Stockholm syndrome in each. Each of these labels used in typical theological language express a "racialized" structure inherent in homes, society, and churches. Peter J. Paris argues for a "the black Christian tradition."

> The tradition that has always been normative for the black churches and the black community is not the so-called Western Christian tradition per se, although this tradition is an important source for blacks. More accurately, the normative tradition for blacks is that tradition governed by the principle of non-racism which we call the black Christian tradition. The terms "Western" and "black" designate two different but very significant

8. Cone, *For My People*, 112.

modifications of Christianity. Since religious experience is always conditioned in important ways by its sociopolitical context, it follows that significant differences in the latter imply corresponding differences in the former. This tradition has been represented as a fundamental principle of criticism justifying and motivating all endeavors by blacks for survival and social transformation.[9]

The "Black Christian tradition" argued by Paris stands in opposition to the Western Christian tradition because the latter represented tradition is rooted in white churches. The breakdown of this relationship was complicated by slavery and perpetuated the superiority of whites over blacks preached through religion as "Godly." Since the inception of the black church, there has always been a perception that theology and sociology must not be in contradiction.

Concomitantly, the white church (notwithstanding the historical slavery connotations), has tended to dictate its concern for prominent causes directly to the black church. The black church then makes those causes its causes in this pre-symbiotic relationship. This white church label is viewed through the lens of Protestant Evangelical Christianity which historically was seen as the mainstream religion for the first century and a quarter of American history. "A racialized society is a society wherein race matters profoundly for differences in life experiences, life opportunities, and social relationships. A racialized society can also be said to be a society that allocates differential economic, political, social, and even psychological rewards to groups along racial lines: lines that are socially constructed."[10] Emerson and Smith have summarized that racism, in its classical form, has evolved out of American thought. This progressive metamorphosis of racialization has changed from individualism to institutionalism.

Classically, the racism of Ku Klux Klan ideology of overt hatred and violent action of racial superiority comes to mind. It is a reminder of how individuals lynched and tortured black people and burned their homes. The burning cross is a symbol of this type

9. Paris, *The Social Teaching of the Black Churches*, 10–11.

10. Emerson and Smith, *Divided by Faith*, 7.

of racism. Based on social surveys with questions that reflect this type of mindset, sociologist have concluded that in present day logic, these type of people are declining in percentage with respect to the total population and have concluded that prejudicial racism of the individual type is on the decline.[11] Therefore, Emerson and Smith have come to the same conclusion as other sociologists and authors like Tim Wise and Michelle Alexander. Wise argues the election of a black President did not disprove the reality of racism while Alexander declares the discrimination of open racism has morphed into an affront of a perception of color blindness.

Socio-theologically, how far has the church come since the Civil Rights Movement? The church continues to give the perception of cognitive dissonance with regard to race in America. The separate by equal Jim Crow laws have infiltrated the theological make up of Christianity—say it ain't so! Complacency in church rhetoric with regards to race maintains the status quo. The church wears ceremonial robes of invisibility while silenced with the voices of complacency and tolerance un-vitalized by antiquity. Apathetic ignorance holds the church sympathetic to the captor (racism)—an evil the church should not tolerate. In 1907, Dubois made the following observation, "The church aided and abetted the Negro slave trade; the church was the bulwark of American slavery; and the church today is the strongest seat of racial and color prejudice."[12]

Malcolm X made the statement that any religion that does not allow him to fight for the freedom of his people is a religion that should be in hell, "I believe in a religion that believes in freedom. Anytime I have to accept a religion that won't let me fight a battle for my people, I say to hell with that religion." The Stockholm syndrome of religious thought flows from this cry of freedom from within the inner-city. Poverty, injustice, inequality, crime, poor education, and poor employment opportunities have kidnapped the church's power to make a difference. The church is in need of spiritual psychiatric counseling and a renewed transformation of

11. Wellman, *Portraits of White Racism*, xxii.

12. Dubois, "Religion in the South," 171.

minds that will free it from the psychosis of racism. The inner-city is choking from the heavy hands of racialization around its throat that is strangling the life out of its youth. The muffle cry of oppression is not being heard by the church at large.

# CONCLUSION

# CHAPTER 10

# Implications/Applications for the Church

THIS WORK HAS ATTEMPTED to illustrate that although we learn from a variety of theologies, Black Theology is crucial for inner-city spirituality among its black and brown youth. No other praxis seems good enough to address the problems of their cultural environment. Rather than presenting an extended argument of which theology works best when and where, this work illustrated how Holy Hip-hop in conjunction with Black Theology more clearly brings a theological perspective to the problems of social injustice, inequality, and racism. Additionally, it is the purpose of this study to highlight that there is an apparent weakness in both Black Theology and traditional Christian theology in that neither has a rhetoric that speaks to this generation of hip-hop without Holy Hip-hop.

Clearly, while the subjects of racism, mass incarceration, injustice, inequality in education, crime, poverty, unemployment, and other socio-political problems are being calmly discussed elsewhere, there has to be a rhetoric that expresses the anger and frustration that inner-city youth feel over their continuing encounters with new Jim Crow policies. The typical religious answers of "let's pray," or "in the world, but not of it," or just the silence of cooperation and apathy is not sufficient for a generation considered as Civil Rights Movement drop-outs. Black Theology is not enough by itself. Although it offers a rich interpretation of God, Bible, and black history and experience, it falls short in speaking the language of a generation robbed of its history. It fails by itself to respond to the psychological needs of youth who are struggling with oppressive circumstances. "A new civil rights movement cannot be organized around the relics of the earlier system of control if it is to address meaningfully the racial realities of our time. Any racial justice movement, to be successful, must vigorously challenge the public consensus that underlies the prevailing system of control."[1]

In other words, something new has to be developed since the demise of the old Civil Rights regime. The social pathologies of racism protested then has morphed itself into a new form of control that demands a new aggressive challenge. It was Albert Einstein who originated the often repeated definition of insanity when he stated, "Insanity is doing the same thing over and over again and expecting different results."[2] It becomes obvious that America cannot continue to keep on this path of socialized racism and expect "God bless America" to become answered prayer.

America would like to think of itself as living out the color-blind dream of Martin Luther King Jr., however it is apparent that America is really living the nightmare of Malcolm X. "In individuals, insanity is rare; but in groups, parties, nations and epochs, it is the rule."[3] The social barriers that were present during the Civil Rights movement have not been removed, but have in fact been refocused and re-strengthened into an upgrade form of oppression. These barriers are not only noticeable on social levels but are also seen in the church.

Most young hip-hoppers are faced with life changing choices that demand survival take priority over salvation. They must make a daily decision between the profane and the sacred, life and death. This leaves no time for an irrelevant gospel. In the inner-city, what frequently passes as "the gospel" is associated with a generational slavery mindset that was inherited from our ancestors. This mindset

1. Alexander, *The New Jim Crow*, 223.

2. Howes, "The Definition of Insanity is. . . Perseverance vs. Perseveration." According to Ryan Howes, the quote has been attributed to Einstein, Ben Franklin and Mark Twain. Sources commonly attribute the quote to Einstein in his Letters to Solovine: 1906-1955 although no one seems to be able to produce a page from that volume that holds the quote.

3. Nietzsche, Friedrich. *Beyond Good and Evil*. 156.

is rejected by a new "black consciousness." It must be remembered that "black consciousness" comes from black thought. In other words, according to Wilmore, black religious thought and Black Theology together share a simple reality: an indestructible belief in freedom, a freedom born in the African environment which includes aspects of black life and culture, which non-black scholars would call secular, non-Christian, and sometimes anti-Christian.

Black Theology is not a religion or the preaching of another gospel; rather, Black Theology is a representation of that worldview that sees God through those social conditions that shape faith. Black history is rarely taught in the school curriculum and neither is Black Theology taught in the church; therefore, youth are not getting any type of black history; secular or sacred. Black youth, in particular, are not given a theological history of their identity in biblical scripture, nor are they told how God has always been with a race of people who are oppressed. Nothing is said to them about their origins as a people, neither in church nor the secular classroom, therefore, all they have is their present. Black Theology can benefit Holy Hip-hop because it brings in biblical history; it brings in a prophetic revelation of who oppressed peoples have been through scripture. Holy Hip-hop can communicate that to a younger generation who do not understand those origins.

Black Theology is teaching. It teaches young people how and why to worship God. That is to say, it is a method of communication, a method of evangelism that can be realized in the inner-city context because people can recognize *who* they are and *whose* they are through their experience. This is the symbiotic relationship between Holy Hip-hop and Black Theology. Holy Hip-hop teaches young people how to praise God as to what He has done through their relationship with Him. The expression of that union is in the power of the music and its ability to produce and/or reconcile the religious experience with identity through rap, the universal language of hip-hop. Christian rap is greater than the commercialized gangsta music that revels in misogyny, materialism, and criminal imaginations; moreover, Christian rap is not an avenue for chaos.

It is, in fact, a prophetic voice of protest and also foretells of God's cooperation with this generation.

A theological review of the necessity of Black Theology and Holy Hip-hop working jointly together will create a new mindset that is appropriately needed at this time. Hip-hop music (especially rap) is an enigma to those who "listen" to its content. Hip-hop rap sometimes takes a hard look at the confusion that exists as inner-city people try to live their lives through adverse perspectives and experiences. Hip-hop music (especially rap) bonds people together and separates them at the same time as it documents the weaknesses in our daily lives and interactions with one another.

Holy Hip-hop also has a platform of activism: rap. Inherent to the nature of rap, there is a duality in which hip-hoppers must take cognizance of what is happening in this form of expression. There is a bitter line between the sacred and profane in which identity can be lost or at best confused in the inner-city context. Herein is the dilemma of the rap lyric: it has the power to celebrate a consciousness of black respectability or lend itself to a consciousness of anti-social pathology. The prophetic voices of the civil rights era are silent in the age of the new prophetic voices of this hip-hop generation. The old nihilistic prophetic voices that spoke from generations past have no "game" in the reality of where hip-hoppers are now.

For the Hispanic, Holy Hip-hop makes sense to angry young Latinas/os. It enables like minds to understand in a common conscientiousness of shared experiences that are not uncommon to each. When used in the context of church, Holy Hip-hop provides a way for this culture to understand the church does not reject them and offers a way for relief from drugs, gang violence, domestic abuse, police brutality, inequality in the justice system, and abandonment.

Socialized racism is disguised in the political laws and policies that make the inner-city a new concentration camp with holocaustic results conceptualized in the schools and prisons. The back lash of the old Jim Crow against the Civil Rights movement has become "resurrected" with a new face that operates as collective parts held together systematically and strategically to maintain itself as America's worst evil; a new Jim Crow; different look but the same eyes.

Culture and religion have most always been seen as a broken marriage with "irreconcilable differences." Black Theology has the ability to retool past issues for a new audience (hip-hop) because it restates a passionate understanding of biblical history pointing out that oppression is not a new thing to God. The crimes of oppression since slavery demonstrate the brutality and barbarism of racism, and Christian participation in that cruelty magnifies the worldview of this culture that all religion is complicit in that oppression. Black Theology, therefore, must be revived in the language of the ecclesiastical discourse to unbalance the power of racism experienced in the cultural context of the inner-city and lived in the lives of this hip-hop generation.

The social complexities of inner-city life that lead to questions about God's involvement with injustice and inequality are examined from the theological perspectives of Habakkuk and Job. Throughout biblical scripture, men and women have asked the question, "why?" It is a natural question that demands a supernatural answer. Believers have asked this common question in an effort to find some theologically-based understanding of personal and corporate crises. The biblical-theological section of this book is concerned with two key conceptions in relationship to God and the inner-city experience: trust and faith. From the questions asked of Habakkuk and Job, a clear inner-city perspective of trust and faith in God is identifiable. Is the inner-city the victim of an oppressor as envisioned by Habakkuk or is it receiving punishment in accordance with the temporal retribution theology applied to Job? The answers to these questions (or at least an attempt to understand the nature of the questions) help to determine how Black Theology can assist in the space between the question and God's answer, because in that space is a test of faith.

Black Theology and Holy Hip-hop found each other in the oppressive consciousness of those who believed that freedom is found in Jesus Christ. Black Theology teaches about the other worldliness of earthy atrocities as Holy Hip-hop articulates that language. Many people who are black, brown, and poor do not have a "champion" who speaks on their behalf. Now, through the efforts of this project, Black Theology is joined to a voice (rap) and the voice is joined to a purpose (theology). On its own merit, Black Theology began to sound like any other religion to this hip-hop generation. The sanctimonious platitudes of pastors made them all seem the same. Who can "pray" when the entire world is against you and every day is just another day in the hood that forces everyone to survive like animals. With this marriage, there is now a bridge between the sacred and profane, and there is not an all-or-nothing conversion necessary to realize Jesus; in fact, as young people come to faith through Black Theology utilizing the voice of Holy Hip-hop, *Jesuz* can be found and experienced.

What are the challenges that lie ahead for the church with regard to the sins of racism, slavery, injustice, and inequality? How does a theology of the Cross inform a response to oppression? Is there any comparison to be drawn between the death of Christ on the Cross and the lynching (unarmed killing) of black men, women, and children in American history? A historical-theological agreement demonstrates how a present and future liberating theology responds to a Willie Lynch Curse of an evangelical inner-city mindset and its ongoing effects. "As long as the mind is enslaved, the body can never be free. Psychological freedom, a firm sense of self-esteem, is the most powerful weapon against the long night of physical slavery."[4]

Inner-city "Pharisees" are leaders who fail to reach inner-city youth because they have no training in hermeneutical contextualization outside of their narrow tradition and what they perceive as "church." As a result, what is real outside the church does not reflect what is inside the church; making Christianity unrealistic. The truth about life becomes confused in the mediocrity of non-stimulating intellectual dogma with traditional cobwebs of antiquity; making biblical truth at best irrelevant and at worst a lie to the reality of inner-city life. The church in the inner-city and

---

4. King, *Where Do We Go from Here?* 44.

anywhere else cannot continue to duplicate what is known not to work, neither can the church allow itself to fall into obscurity because it is not relevant; old words do not produce new actions and tradition does not produce change. As a result, God appears to be more in the "other" world while alienated from the affairs of "this" world.

The challenge is clear; theologians are charged to break the fall of racist sin and fulfill the mandate of righteous dominion over its power by the grace of God. A theological task awaits those with a firm conviction that powers and principalities in high places will not circumvent God in His redeeming work of the Cross of Jesus. "There comes a time when one must take a position that is neither safe, nor politic, nor popular, but he must take it because conscience tells him it is right."[5] The three-fold foci of this book are Black Theology, Holy Hip-hop, and their conjoint working together to combat America's deadliest sin: racism. The emerging challenge to traditionalism portents a radical shift in approach to the inner-city. The ignorance that surrounds Black Theology and Holy Hip-hop must be dispelled; and to God be the glory through the redemptive work of the Cross of Christ.

The Holy Ghost dance is an indication of God's presence taking over the flesh and the mind lending itself to the power of God's Spirit inwardly. It is an outward action of surrender to the goodness of God in the lives of believers. Worship surrenders our spirit to God because of who He is and praise is our surrender to God for what He has and continues to do in our lives. There must be a balance of praise and worship; and if the balance is imperfect in any way, God is not glorified. However, to many who witness this dance, there is a degree of skepticism that this form of worship is fleshy and contrived. It is an "old" form of worship started by the older generation of church. Furthermore, when young people of the millennial generation witness the "Holy Ghost Dance" red flags of distrust and fakeness become evident. Young millennials must be taught that dancing with the Spirit is a form of worship even though evil tries to corrupt it with un-godly fleshy expressions.

5. King, *A Testament of Hope*, 276.

The Holy Ghost got a new dance and it is a new dance of freedom upon the floor of oppression. This dance occurs in the hearts of those seeking the freedom and liberty promised by God to those who believe. This dance is in concert with God's redemptive plan of salvation while stepping to the music of the passion of Christ's Cross. The Holy Ghost got a new dance that is bigger than the off-beats of racism, incarceration, inequality, injustice, and poverty. It is reminiscent of a child standing on the feet of God as He teaches His children how to dance with His Spirit and purpose. Black Theology teaches the movement of the dance to the socially relevant rhythmic lyrics Holy Hip-hop.

# Bibliography

Alexander, Michelle. *The New Jim Crow: Mass Incarceration in the Age of Colorblindness*. New York: The New, 2012.

Andersen, Francis I., et al., *The Anchor Bible: Habakkuk*. Vol. 25. New York: Doubleday, 2001.

Basler, Roy P., ed. *The Collected Works of Abraham Lincoln*. Vol. 2, *Speech at Peoria, Illinois October 16, 1854*. New York: American Historical Review, 1953.

Beckett, Katherine. *Making Crime Pay: Law and Order in Contemporary American Politics (Studies in Crime and Public Policy)*. New York: Oxford University Press, 1997.

Bennett, Lerone. *The Challenge of Blackness*. Detroit, Michigan: Johnson, 1972.

Blum, Edward J., and Paul Harvey. *The Color of Christ: The Son of God and the Saga of Race in America*. North Carolina: North Carolina, 2014.

"Byrne JAG Funding in California." *California NCJP*. http://www.ncjp.org/states/ca?vdt=glossary%7Cpage_2. (accessed January 30, 2014).

Carver, Joseph M. "Love and Stockholm Syndrome: The Mystery of Loving an Abuser." (accessed January 20, 2014). http://drjoecarver.makeswebsites.com/clients/49355/File/love_and_stockholm_syndrome.

Cone, James. *A Black Theology of Liberation*. 20th ed. New York: Orbis Books, 2010.

———. *Black Theology and Black Power*. 5th ed. Maryknoll, New York: Orbis Books, 1997.

———. *The Cross and the Lynching Tree*. New York, New York: Orbis Books, 2011.

———. *For My People: Black Theology and the Black Church, Where Have We Been and Where Are We Going?* New York: Orbis Books, 1984.

Cooper, Joel M. *Cognitive Dissonance: 50 Years of a Classic Theory*. California: Sage Publications, 2007.

Davis, Angela. "Masked Racism." In *Sing, Whisper, Shout, Pray: Feminist Visions for a Just World*, edited by Jaqui Alexander, et al., 50–57. Canada: EdgeWork Books, 2003.

De Haan, Richard W. *Song in the Night.* Grand Rapids: Radio Bible Class (booklet), 1969.

Dubois, W.E. Burghardt. "Does the Negro Need Separate Schools?" *Journal of Negro Education* Volume IV No. 3, (July, 1935) 328–35.

———. "Religion in the South." In *The Negro in the South,* Edited by Booker T. Washington and W.E.B. Dubois, 212. New York: Citadel, 1970.

Duncan, Birt L. "Differential Social Perception and Attributes of Intergroup Violence: Testing the Lower Limits of Stereotyping of Blacks." *Journal of Personality and Social Psychology* (1976) 590–98.

Dyson, Michael E. *Between God and Gangsta Rap: Bearing Witness to Black Culture.* New York: Oxford, 1996.

———. *Holler If You Hear Me.* New York: Basic Civitas, 2001.

Edelman, Peter, Harry J. Holzer, and Paul Offner. *Reconnecting Disadvantaged Young Men.* Washington D.C.: The Urban Institute, 2006.

Education Trust-West. *At A Crossroads: A Comprehensive Picture of how African-American Youth Fare in Los Angeles County Schools.* Oakland, California, 2013.

Ellis, Richard J. *To the Flag: The Unlikely History of the Pledge of Allegiance.* Kansas: University Press, 2005.

Elliston, Edgar J., and J. Timothy Kauffman. *Developing Leaders for Urban Ministries.* New York: Peter Lang, 2000.

Emerson, Michael O., and Christian Smith. *Divided by Faith: Evangelical Religion and the Problem of Race in America.* New York: Oxford University Press, 2000.

Entwisle, Doris, Karl L. Alexander, and Linda Steffel Olson. *Children, Schools, and Inequality.* Boulder, Colorado: West View, 1997.

Epstein, Kelly Kitty. *A Different View of Urban Schools: Civil Rights, Critical Race Theory and Unexplored Realities (Counterpoints: Studies in the Postmodern Theory of Education).* New York: Lang, 2006.

Feagin, Joe R., and Melvin P. Sikes. *Living with Racism: The Black Middle-Class Experience.* Boston: Beacon, 1994.

Fletcher, Garth Baker. *Xodus: An African American Male Journey.* Minneapolis: Fortress Press, 1996.

Gilbreath, Edward. *Birmingham Revolution: Martin Luther King Jr.'s Epic Challenge to the Church.* Downers Grove, Illinois: Intervarsity, 2013.

Grimes, Katie. "The Cross and the Lynching Tree." *Women in Theology Blog.* April 22, 2011. Accessed August 4, 2014, http://www.womenintheology.org/.

Guisbond, Lisa, Monty Neill, and Bob Schaeffer. *NCLB's Lost Decade for Educational Progress: What Can We learn from this Policy Failure?* Fair Test National Center for Fair and Open Testing. Boston, January 2012.

Gutierrez, Gustavo. *On Job: God-Talk and the Suffering of the Innocent.* New York: Orbis Books, 1987.

———. *The Power of the Poor in History.* New York: Orbis Books, 1983.

Hammond, Linda Darling. "Inequality and the Right to Learn: Access to Qualified Teachers in California's Public Schools." *Teachers College Record* (2004) 1936–66.

Hiebert, T. *The New Interpreter's Bible: A Commentary in Twelve Volumes*, vol. 7, *The Book of Habakkuk*. Nashville: Abingdon, 1996.

Hodge, Daniel White. *The Soul of Hip-hop: Rims, Timbs and a Cultural Theology*. Downers Grove, Illinois: Inter Varsity, 2010.

Hopkins, Dwight. *Introducing Black Theology of Liberation* Maryknoll, New York: Orbis Books, 1999.

Howes, Ryan. "The Definition of Insanity Is: Perseverance vs. Perseveration." *Psychology Today* (July 27, 2009). <http://www.psychologytoday.com/blog/in-therapy/200907/the-definition-insanity-is>.

Jerigan, David, and Lori Dorfman. "Visualizing America's Drug Problems: An Ethnographic Content Analysis of Illegal Drug Stories on the Nightly News." *Contemporary Drug Problems* 23 (1996) 169, 188.

King, Martin Luther., Jr. *Strength to Love*. Minneapolis: Fortress, 2010.

———. *A Testament of Hope: The Essential Writings and Speeches* (New York: Harper One, 2003).

———. *Where Do We Go from Here?* A speech delivered at the 11th Annual SCLC Convention in Atlanta, Georgia, August 16, 1967. In *A Call to Conscience: The Landmark Speeches of Martin Luther King, Jr.*, edited by Clayborne Carson and Kris Shepard. New York: IPM/Warner Books, 2001.

Kitwana, Bakari. *The Hip-Hop Generation: Young Blacks and the Crisis in African-American Culture*. New York: Basic Civitas Books, 2002.

Kunjufu, Jawanza. *Countering the Conspiracy to Destroy Black Boys*, vol. 2. Chicago: African American Images, 1986.

Lynch, Willie. *The Making of a Slave*. U.S.A.: BN Publishing, 2009.

Mauer, Marc. *Race to Incarcerate*, Rev. Ed. New York: The New, 2006.

Mauer, Marc, and Ryan King. *A 25-Year Quagmire: The "War on Drugs" and It's Impact on American Society*. Washington, DC: Sentencing Project, 2007.

Meares, Tracy. "Charting Race and Class Differences in Attitudes Toward Drug Legalization and Law Enforcement: Lessons for Federal Criminal Law." 1 *Buffalo Criminal Law Review* (1997) 474.

Meier, Deborah, et al., eds. *Many Children Left Behind: How the No Child Left Behind Act Is Damaging Our Children and Our Schools*. Boston: Beacon, 2004.

Morrow, Alvin. *Breaking the Curse of Willie Lynch: The Science of Slave Psychology*. Missouri: Rising Sun, 2003.

Moss III, Otis. "Real Big: The Hip Hop Pastor as Postmodern Prophet." In *The Gospel Remix: Reaching the Hip Hop Generation*, edited by Ralph C. Watkins, 110. Valley Forge: Judson, 2007.

Niebuhr, Reinhold. *The Children of the Light and the Children of Darkness*. New York: Charles Scribner's Sons, 1944.

Nietzsche, Friedrich. *Beyond Good and Evil.* Ireland: Millennium Publications, 2014.

Ogbar, Jeffrey O.G. *Hip-Hop Revolution: The Culture and Politics of Rap.* Lawrence, University of Kansas, 2007.

Page, Clarence. "'The Plan:' A Paranoid View of Black Problems." *Dover Herald,* (Feb 23, 1990).

Paris, Peter J. *The Social Teaching of the Black Churches.* Philadelphia: Fortress, 1985.

Pavlov, I. P. *Lectures on Conditioned Reflexes,* translated by W. H. Gantt. London: Allen and Unwin, 1941.

———. *Selected Works,* translated by S. Koshtoyants. Moscow: Foreign Languages House, 1955.

———. *The Work of the Digestive Glands,* translated by William Henry Thomas. London: Griffin, 1928.

Perry, Imani. *Prophets of the Hood: Politics and Poetics in Hip-Hop.* United States: Duke University Press, 2004.

Price, Frederick K.C. *Race, Religion and Racism.* Vol.1. Los Angeles: Faith One, 1999.

Raboteau, Albert J. *Slave Religion: The "Invisible Institution" in the Antebellum South.* New York: Oxford, 2004.

Reeves, Jimmie, and Richard Campbell, *Cracked Coverage: Television News, the Anti-Cocaine Crusade and the Reagan Legacy.* Durham, NC: Duke University Press, 1994.

Sanchez-Walsh, Arlene M. *Latino Pentecostal Identity: Evangelical Faith, Self and Society.* Chi Chester, New York: Columbia University Press, 2003.

Smith, Ralph L., et al. *World Biblical Commentary: Micah-Malachi.* Waco, Texas: Thomas Nelson, 1984.

Spencer, Jon Michael. Preface to *The Theology of American Popular Music,* a special issue of *Black Sacred Music: A Journal of Theomusicology* 3, no.2 (Fall 1989).

Stallings, James O. *Telling the Story: Evangelism in Black Churches.* Valley Forge, Pennsylvania: Judson, 1988.

Szykowny, Rick. "No Justice, No Peace: An Interview with Jerome Miller." *The Free Library,* http://thefreelibrary.com/No+justice%2c+no+peace%3b+an+interview+with+Jerome+Miller.-a014713826 (Jan–Feb 1994).

Twain, Mark. "The United States of Lyncherdom." In *Collected Tales, Sketches, Speeches, & Essays 1891-1910,* edited by Louis J. Budd, 479. New York: Liberty of America, 1992.

Watkins, Ralph C. *The Gospel Remix: Reaching the Hip Hop Generation.* King of Prussia, New Jersey: Judson, 2007.

Wellman, David T. *Portraits of White Racism.* New York: Cambridge University Press, 1977.

West, Cornell. *Prophetic Thought in Postmodern Times.* Monroe, Maryland: Common Courage, 1993.

———. *Race Matters.* Boston: Beacon, 1993.

White, Joseph L. *The Psychology of Blacks: An Afro-American Perspective,* New Jersey: Prentice-Hall, 1984.

Wilson, William Julius. *When Work Disappears: The World of the New Urban Poor.* New York: Vintage, 1997.

Wise, Tim. *Dear White America.* San Francisco: City Lights Books, 2012.

Woods, Forrest. *Arrogance of Faith.* New York: Alfield A. Knopf, 1991.

Woodson, Carter G., and Willie Lynch. *The Mis-Education of the Negro.* New York: Classic Books America, 2009.

Made in the USA
Middletown, DE
13 June 2019